D1576381

I2087363

THE GREEK ISLANDS

THE GREEK ISLANDS

text: Renée Grimaud photographs: Patrick de Wilde

SANDWELL LIBRARY & INFORMATION SERVICE	
I2087363	
Bertrams	16.03.06
914.500222	£20.00

MACEDONIA

ADRIATIC

ITALY

ALBANIA

Thessaloniki

Corfu (Kerkyra)

Paxi

Skiathos

IONIAN SEA

Skop

I O N I A N
I S L A N D S

Lefkadha (Lefkas)

Ev

Ithaki

Kefallonia

ATHEN

Salamina

Zante (Zakynthos)

Angistri

Eg

Pe

Idr

Spetses *A R G O -*
S A R O N I
I S L A N D

MEDITERRANEAN

Kythira

0	20		100 km
0	12½		62½ miles

BULGARIA

BLACK SEA

Istanbul •

SEA OF MARMARA

Thassos

Samothraki

*ISLANDS
OF THE
AEGEAN*

Imbros (Gokceada)

Limnos

Ayios Efstratios

PORADES

Alonissos

Lesvos

TURKEY

Skyros

Psara

Hios

AEGEAN SEA

Andhros

Samos

Tinos

Ikaria

Kea

Mykonos

Syros

Kythnos

Dhilos

Patmos

Leros

CYCLADES

Dhonoussa

Serifos

Paros

Kalymnos

Naxos

Kos

Sifnos

Koufonissi

D O D E C A N E S E

Kimolos

Skhinoussa

Keros

Amorgos

Iraklia

Sikinos

Milos

Ios

Astypalea

Nissyros

Symi

Folegandhros

Tilos

Santorini
(Thira)

Anafi

Rodhos
(Rhodes)

SEA OF CRETE

Karpathos

K R I T I (C R E T E)

Kassos

The Greek Islands have long been a source of fascination, and back in classical times were the inspiration for the *Odyssey*, the masterpiece of Greece's greatest epic poet, Homer. Their total area amounts to nearly 9,700 sq miles (25,000 km²), and there are more than 3,000 of them, if you include many that are tiny dots scarcely visible on a map.

They were captured by pirates, regularly plundered, and dominated in turn by the Genoese, the Venetians (whose occupation was, economically speaking, the most beneficial), the Ottoman Turks, the French, the British (who constructed road systems, for example in the Ionian Islands), the Italians and the Germans. Some of the islands, including the Ionian and in particular Kefallonia and Zakynthos, were devastated in 1953 by an earthquake from which they might never have recovered, had it not been for the tenacity of their inhabitants. Valiantly, they have resisted every crisis. Today they have to cope with invasions of tourists, putting up with the construction, alas, of ghastly apartment blocks and the peculiarly tasteless hotels designed for the hordes that appear in the high season. But the beaches remain beautiful, especially when empty! And those transparent blue waters!

The islands have 1,600,000 residents, or 15% of the nation's total population, a third of them on Crete. The number of inhabited islands is just over a hundred, but some are so small that they are home to only a few dozen people. Tourism apart, the islands are far from productive as sources of employment, even if a few have retained their fishing and farming activities. Many suffer from regular depopulation, though there have been happy exceptions: Corfu (Greek: Kerkyra), for instance, saw its population increase from 97,000 to 107,000 between 1981 and 2001.

For a long time, economic underdevelopment resulted in island populations being dispersed to the four winds. Some were forced into exile in North America and Australia, and then from 1947, after the civil war, others sought refuge in

the communist countries, and finally, around 1960, many emigrated to Germany. Following the fall of the Colonels in 1974, the tourist industry encouraged some of the islanders to stay and others to return.

Some islands have a unique experience of emigration. Take Kythira (Cythera), for example, one of the Ionian group, which was the inspiration for a painting by Watteau. Many of its citizens moved to Australia, especially Sydney, at first because of the gold rush in around 1850, but many followed later, lured by this far-distant Eldorado. So numerous have been the emigrants that Kythira is nicknamed 'Kangaroo Island'! Having passed their active lives in Australia, the Greeks often retire to Kythira, where they are recognisable by ... their Bermuda shorts! In Kefallonia, another of the Ionian islands, some villages have reminders of happier days when the young men left their native soil for long voyages at sea, amassing fortunes and returning home to become local benefactors. They provided the means for the construction of municipal buildings and sporting facilities and built the grandest houses in the district for themselves. For the islander, exiled in a faraway land or sailing the seven seas, there is one overriding desire: to return to his home. Such are the ties that bind him to his little piece of land.

The Greek islands have always been the stuff of dreams. They conjure up visions of deep blue water, long, white, sandy beaches, and little harbours where gaily painted boats bob at their moorings and the smell of grilled octopus and *ouzo* (dispensed liberally by the Greeks) drifts in the breeze. There is a tendency to think of the islands as white and blue, but there are others where the predominant hues are green and ochre. We like to imagine them as deserted, but sometimes they are populated – overloaded in fact – with tourists. We may picture Pythagoras, a native of Samos, positing mathematics as the fundamental principal of the universe; Sappho reinventing poetry on Lesvos (classical Lesbos); or El Greco, born at Candia (modern Iraklion) in Crete, toiling at his

masterpieces in Venice and, later, in Spain. The writer Nikos Kazantzakis was also a native of Candia and was buried there in 1957, having paid well-deserved homage to his native island, and the poet Odysseas Elytis lived for many years in Mytilini, his father's birthplace.

The boat is the favourite method of transport in Greece, with thousands of ferries of every size crisscrossing the sea to link the tiny islands. There are a large number of shipping companies, and the routes are very crowded. Even the smallest islands are accessible, even if there is only one boat a week. In such cases, its arrival is eagerly anticipated, as it brings items like mail, newspapers, bottled gas and provisions. In the last few decades new means of transport have made their appearance: hydrofoils and, more recently, catamarans, which, although too small to carry cars, are much quicker. Journey times are often slashed by half.

The departure of a big ferry is always an event. The enormous holds gape wide, swallowing articulated lorries, tourist buses, gleaming 4x4s or big limousines. Watching the lengthy queues waiting to disappear into the ship's bowels, it's hard to imagine they'll all find a place. But it's staggering what the boats can carry. Swarms of tourists mount the steps, instinctively making for various decks, the bars, or, on more luxuriously equipped vessels, the saloons. Up come the anchors, ropes are coiled away, the siren sounds. Away to the isles! People bring out their snacks, set off in search of an iced Nescafé, or sit back and contemplate the seemingly endless sea. Once the coast is in sight – often behind schedule – a kind of frenzy appears to overtake the passengers. Men rush back down to the holds in search of their vehicles, revving the engines well before the boat has docked, and there's a dash for the gangways with everyone clutching armfuls of luggage: the vessel has to be evacuated swiftly ready to put out again for other islands.

The island landscapes provide a fascinating geography lesson. One slope, for instance, may be very gentle, the other steep and rugged, with high mountains in the centre, and even the colour of the rock may vary from one side of the island to the other. Sometimes there are marshy areas, as on Lefkadha or in the south of Corfu. The highest point of an island often boasts a fortress, the relic of Venetian occupation; in olden days, many villages were built as high as possible to protect them from regular pirate raids. Another characteristic of Greek islands is their individuality: each has a personality of its own. Even when islands are not far apart, the atmosphere of each can be remarkably different, whether expressed in the architecture of the houses, the welcome accorded to visitors, or the local customs and accents. One island may be devoted to agriculture, another may have sacrificed everything to tourism, and there are those that manage to maintain a balance between a range of activities. They all possess an overwhelming charm deriving from a way of life unique to the Greeks ...

THE CYCLADES

These are the best known of all the islands, the most photographed, the most visited.

MYKONOS AND DHILOS

The dazzling white that characterises these islands is the result of sunlight reflected on the walls of houses and churches, which the local people scrupulously repaint with fresh, cleansing lime each year before Easter. Even the windmills standing guard on the hills overlooking the sea are white. The dramatic royal blue of church domes and every house door and window, the inspiration for countless photographers, is believed to keep away the mosquitoes. When the *meltemi* – a northerly wind particularly fierce throughout the summer – is blowing, the waters of the Mediterranean glitter like deep blue jewels.

The Cyclades are astonishing in their variety, from those that are unspoilt to tourist hotspots, but they all share certain features. Brutally exposed to the winds, they are clothed only with meagre vegetation clinging to the spiky rocks. The ports are frequently dominated by the tall silhouette of a *castro* built by the Genoese and Venetians who were ever-present here in the Middle Ages. The atmosphere seems like a taste of heaven: windmills, a handful of small boats, wooden tables and chairs, nets hung out to dry, a squid awaiting the grill ... Then there are the ubiquitous cats, drifting between the tables in search of titbits ...

For a long time travellers knew little of Greece apart from the Acropolis and the Cyclades, whose name refers to the circle (Greek: kuklos) which they form around the sacred isle of Dhilos (classical Delos): 39 in all, of which 24 are inhabited. And who has not heard of Mykonos, the most famous of these, where the nightlife has been a legend for thirty years or more? It has countless chapels (at least 365, one for each day of the year), constructed, it is said, by pirates who had made their fortunes; twisting alleys lined with fishermen's dwellings; and whitewashed windmills, blinding in the sunlight – but these have failed to stem the deliberate commercial invasion of this steep and rugged scrap of land. Mykonos has now become – and it seems will ever remain – a mecca for those from all over the globe in search of good times, and an inevitable port of call for cruise ships.

Preceding double page:
Whitewashed windmills, survivors of the many buildings formerly devoted to the flour industry on the Cyclades. They operate mainly between July and September, after the harvests.

Opposite:
Mules are still found everywhere in Greece. Patient and untiring, they are used for conveying merchandise all over Mykonos and are often seen bringing back the grain harvest. They happily cope with twisting roads and steep, narrow alleys, the inescapable result of the island's topography. They also add that vital touch of local colour to everyday life.

Above and opposite page:
Balconies and stairways full of potted
flowers and the brightly painted doors
and windows contrast starkly with
dazzling white walls and the two shades
of marble paving the narrow streets.
This is a common feature of the
Cyclades, islands with an immediately
identifiable personality.

Right:
The pelican is the mascot of Mykonos.
Such is its popularity that its image
appears in many tavernas and cafés.

Separated from Mykonos by a few hundred yards of water is the sacred island of Dhilos (Delos), where, since classical times, no one has been permitted to live or die. It is a paradise for lovers of archaeology and mythology. It was, according to legend, the birthplace of two illustrious gods: the huntress Artemis, and Apollo, god of the Sun, of poetry and music. In the latter's honour, Dhilos was named the 'Shining Isle'. From Mykonos there are daily boat services allowing visitors to explore what was one of the leading religious, cultural and commercial centres of ancient Greece.

Preceding double page:
'Little Venice' is a district of Mykonos by the water's edge which is composed of fine houses once belonging to sea captains from the years of the island's prosperity. You can linger on the café terraces with a glass of ouzo and admire the sunset.

Opposite:

The sanctuary of Dhilos is dominated by the temples towering above what is a vast open-air museum. Wonderful mosaics, some still extremely well preserved, adorn the wealthiest buildings.

Above, left:

This fine bull's head, carved in marble, is decorated with fruits and cornstalks symbolising fertility. It is remarkable for its expressiveness and its excellent state of preservation.

Above, right:

A majestic lion, sculpted from Naxos marble: one of the five beasts lining the terrace beside the sacred lake in the sanctuary of Apollo at Dhilos. Originally there were nine, and they stood guard at the temple of Leto, frozen for ever in the act of roaring. They date from the 7th century BC and are among the most famous examples of Cycladic statuary.

SANTORINI (THIRA)

We now leave Mykonos for Santorini or Thira, the volcanic island shaped like a half-moon, with its black and red cliffs where 580 steps lead up to the principal village overlooking the sea nearly 400 ft (120 m) below. Innumerable earthquakes have considerably altered its appearance: it was some three times larger in classical times. Ferries today sail across what was the volcano's crater, and to arrive by boat is a spectacular experience, as the island towers above the water like an enormous cake dressed with trees, in a series of layers. The climb is enough to discourage visitors, but never fear: there are mules standing by to take the more faint-hearted to the top. And it's worth it. Fira, the capital, provides a sensational view of the approaches and the sea, a vista that benefits particularly from the surrounding geometrical architecture, composed of alternating straight lines and curves, arcades and stairs, with a different outlook wherever you happen to be.

A victim of its own success, the town has witnessed the establishment of an amazing number of exorbitantly expensive shops. Those seeking somewhere quieter can take refuge at Perissa or Kamari, with their black-pebbled beaches, while lovers of the picturesque will opt for Oia, the most beautiful of Santorini's villages, boasting cave-houses, domed churches and breathtaking sunsets. On the way to Kamari, it's worth stopping off at the Wine Museum; Santorini produces a pleasant rosé resembling muscatel. But don't miss the trip to Akrotiri, the Pompeii of the Cyclades, buried under tons of volcanic ash after the eruption that shook the island around 1,500 BC. When it was excavated in 1967, frescoes were discovered whose colours retain an extraordinary freshness ...

Fortunately a mule is on hand to take you up the 580 steps leading to the citadel of Santorini. If he could speak, this one, with his colourful harness, could tell many a tale about the tourists he's carried up to the island's summit. For those brave enough to try, the best way is to make the ascent on foot: you can then stop where and when you want and admire one of the most breathtaking panoramas of the Cyclades. There is also a cable car.

Preceding double page:
With its white or blue domes and its whitewashed houses
rising on successive terraces cut into the volcanic cliff,
Fira resembles a mosaic made from two colours.
The present town dates only from 1956, rebuilt when

a violent earthquake ravaged the island – not the
first, by any means. The most cataclysmic was
without doubt that of c.1500 BC, in the Minoan
era, which left Santorini with its present-day
crescent shape.

In Fira: windmills and houses stretching over the summit, springing from heaps of dark brown petrified lava. Some 890 ft (270 m) below, the waters of the approaches are so deep that ships cannot anchor there. This is the caldera, a gigantic crater created by the explosion of the volcano in antiquity, a time when the inhabitants nicknamed Santorini Kalliste: 'Most Beautiful One'.

In Fira, a tiny street named after St Minas, with a church of the same name, links the Orthodox northern town and the Catholic area in the south. From there you can admire those sunsets that have made Santorini's reputation. The island's beaches consist not of fine sand but ash hurled out by the volcano 3,500-odd years ago, so the water appears darker here than elsewhere.

AMORGOS

It was the making of the film *The Big Blue* that, in 1987, suddenly turned the spotlight on Amorgos. Until then, the most easterly of the Cyclades, after its hour of glory during the Cycladic civilisation, had served as a place of exile – though who would have even thought of trying to escape from this long tongue of land surrounded by cliffs and hills and marooned in the very midst of the Aegean? Once the director Luc Besson and his team had left, the almost virgin island, with its rough and rocky paths and some astonishing vistas, became the haunt of ramblers. The views are particularly impressive at Eyiali, the island's second port, in the north. The town is built on terraces above a superb bay whose beach is ideal for lazy days in the sun; three villages are perched high above it, forming a sort of amphitheatre overflowing with luxuriant vegetation. In the south, Hora, the island's chief town, is built around a rock; a labyrinth of tiny, stepped streets, vaulted passages and windmills supply a fantastic backdrop. Nestling against a cliff, the monastery of Hozoviotissas hangs some 1,000 ft (300 m) above the clearest waters of the whole island! Founded in 1088 by the emperor Alexis Comnenus, it houses a collection of extremely precious manuscripts and some glorious icons.

It is hardly surprising that cruise ships choose to call at Amorgos, as it just cries out to be explored. After a bathe in its turquoise waters, those who enjoy walking are spoiled for choice, as a well-signposted network of paths covers the whole island. It's also worth checking out Hora, which has a rich archaeological museum; Eyiali; and particularly Langadha, the most delightful of the island's villages.

SYROS

Syros, delightful in its own right, is the administrative capital of the Cyclades. For a long time it was known only to the Greeks, but has now become appreciated by foreign tourists, who are discovering a traditional island with its typically Cycladean architecture. For several centuries two communities – Orthodox and Catholic – have been living peacefully side by side on Syros; their churches are built on the twin hills of Ermoupoli, the island's capital. On one stands the Orthodox church of Anastassi, founded in 1821 after the arrival of refugees from the massacre on Hios, while on the other is located the Catholic bishopric of Ano Syros, whose cathedral (St George) is perched on top of a rugged crag. The square known as Platia Miaouli, lined by splendid palm trees and paved all over, accommodates the town hall, and is considered one of the most harmonious neoclassical compositions of all Greek architecture. When dusk falls, it becomes the stage for a curious ballet. Dressed in their best, the locals promenade back and forth greeting any acquaintances they meet. This is the *peripato* or *volta*, which, like the *passeggiata* in Italy or the Spanish *paseo*, is a Mediterranean custom deeply rooted in traditional culture. Syros is also famous for its nougat and Turkish delight – sold throughout Greece – and for its small turnovers made with white cheese and honey.

Clinging to the cliffs is the monastery of Hozoviotissas, which the botanist Pitton de Tournefort, visiting Amorgos in the early 1700s, described as 'a wardrobe built onto the base of a terrifying rock face'. It takes some reaching, but when you get there, it's fantastic! Inside, the katholicon is a treasure-house of sumptuous icons, and a small museum in the undercroft gives an idea of daily life in the monastery. From the exterior, there is an awesome view down to the sea almost vertically below.

MILOS

Milos, like Tinos, is a major centre for the worship of the Virgin Mary. On 15 August huge numbers of the faithful converge on the island, the origin of the celebrated armless sculpture *Venus de Milo* now in the Louvre, Paris. Discovered in 1820 by a peasant near the village of Kastro, it was bought by the Marquis de Rivière, the French ambassador to Constantinople, who made a gift of it to Louis XVIII. But the marble from which the statue is made was not quarried locally: it most likely came from Paros or Naxos, other islands of the Cyclades. Milos has always been exploited for different minerals – formerly obsidian and nowadays kaolin – because of its volcanic origins. As for the tourists, they exploit the coastline dotted with some seventy beaches and the peaceful charm of little fishing ports like Klima or Apollonia, typical of the Cyclades, and almost like Greece in microcosm.

TINOS

Nicknamed the Orthodox Lourdes, Tinos also celebrates the Panayia Evangelistria (Feast of the Assumption) on 15 August. The identically named church stands on the spot where an icon of the Virgin with miraculous healing powers was discovered. The story goes that, in 1823, the Virgin appeared to a nun in her sleep, telling her where to find the sacred image. Thousands of pilgrims disembark from special charter boats for the occasion, the most pious mounting the steps to the church on their knees. The icon of the Virgin, which occupies a prominent place in the church during the rest of the year surrounded by hundreds of thank offerings, is carried through the town by the faithful as a sign of their devotion.

But Tinos is also the land of sculptors, whose chisels, since classical times, have carved out astonishing figures from the translucent marble. The existence of two quarries on the island has been a continuing encouragement to islanders to take up the craft; they claim their skills were passed on by Phidias, who produced the sculptures for the Parthenon! According to their story, during a voyage through the Mediterranean, he was obliged to put in at the island, and while there he gave the natives a few tips.

Hundreds of thank offerings – moving examples of popular faith – line the walls of the Panayia Evangelistria. Other more extraordinary items are found there: an orange tree fashioned of gold and silver, for instance, presented by pilgrims whose prayers were answered. The building, which dates from the War of Independence, is in the neoclassical style and dominates Tinos Town.

*In Greece, religion is an integral part of
daily life. In a country where 97% of the
population are Orthodox, traditions remain
strong. Religious festivals are enthusiastically
celebrated by large crowds, with all the usual
symbolic items – medallions, crosses, icons –
on sale everywhere, even by the roadside.*

Inland Tinos has remained very rustic, with its scattering of typical Cycladean villages, their walls freshly whitewashed every year and their little streets full of bright colours. The stony and arid nature of the island restricts agriculture to the level of smallholdings. On the coast, the few beaches guarantee peace and quiet to those who know where to find them.

To enjoy the dovecotes that are a speciality of Tinos, you need to visit the villages at the island's centre. There you will find some very unusual architecture as well: the main street is often vaulted, forming passages known as *kamares*, paved with slabs of schist. And there are no fewer than 1,300 quadrangular towers, the finest being in the valley of Tarambados. They were built by the Venetians, who, between the thirteenth and sixteenth centuries, introduced the breeding of doves to the islands. The towers are whitewashed, have flat roofs, and their architectural decoration includes small columns, rose windows, finials, triangles, diamonds and honeycomb shapes, the overall effect being reminiscent of lacework.

Preceding double page, above,
and opposite:
The dovecotes (peristerionas) of Tinos
are unique to the island, their shape
recalling that of miniature Venetian
towers. The lower level serves as a
storage area, while the top storey,
often crowned with finials, houses the
birds. With their elaborate and highly
original decoration, these structures
are emblems of Tinos, whose authorities
are trying to preserve them from the
ravages of the weather.

NAXOS

Naxos, largest of the Cyclades, is still a well-preserved island abounding in fertile valleys with their rows of vines, fruit trees and olives. Its shores glitter with marble, the lucent stone that has given birth to so many works of art. In mythology, it was here on Naxos that Theseus abandoned Ariadne, daughter of King Minos, on his way back from Crete after slaying the Minotaur. The beautiful princess was consoled in her despair by Dionysos, who obtained permission from Zeus to make her his bride, and throughout antiquity the island was sacred to the god of grapes and wine.

Naxos was also the centre of a flourishing Cycladic civilisation, a few remarkable relics of which can be admired at the Archaeological Museum in Hora, the main town. Preserved, too, near the entrance to the harbour, is the monumental gate of an archaic temple – quite rare, and so worthy of note. Travellers who dream of a Greek island as pictured in glossy magazines will be drawn to Naxos. The villages possess everything that makes Greek life attractive: a small square, with a bushy tree, and one or more cafés where, at the day's end, the locals meet to gossip or play backgammon. Damrionas, Apiranthos, Apollonia are variations on the theme.

PAROS

After so many delights, the next step is to take the boat for Paros, just opposite Naxos – but it's best to wait until after the high season! In summer, the invasion of tourists effectively masks the island's beauty. There are superb Byzantine churches here, like Ekatondapiliani at Parikia, lovely villages (Naoussa and Lefkes, for instance) and enchanting beaches – and of course the ancient marble quarries which were once the source of the island's reputation.

Dating from the seventeenth century, the monastery of Longovardhas on Paros is an important spiritual centre possessing a library full of precious volumes, which the staff are willing to show visitors on request. It is also a highly active sanctuary, where the monks not only produce wine and cultivate the land, but devote much time to painting icons.

Naoussa, on Paros, is a small, picturesque town whose narrow, white streets, designed to protect locals from pirates and the wind, lead down to a traditional little harbour. Old fishermen can still be seen there mending their nets. Every year on 23 August the town hosts a festival in which 100 caïques stage a mock combat commemorating the islanders' struggle against Barbarossa's pirates; the event culminates in dances and music.

The Cyclades have their own way of life,
as here on Paros, where mopeds offer the
easiest form of transport, able to thread their
way among the tiny village streets without
causing traffic jams. Don't leave Paros without
a visit to the Valley of the Butterflies, in the
west, home to thousands of Jersey tiger moths
during the breeding season (May to August).

Opposite, top:
Hanging from a bar, freshly caught octopus
dry in the sun. Later, they will be grilled over
a wood fire and eaten with a slice of lemon
and a round of bread.

Left:
The monastery of Longovardhas, on the road to Naoussa, an architectural medley of curves and straight lines. Paros boasts several monasteries, including Ekatondapiliani, the largest, in the capital Parikia, as well as the convent called Moni Khristou tou Dhassous, accommodating 100 women.

ANDHROS

Andhros, the most northerly of the Cyclades and one of the largest at nearly 150 square miles (380 km^2), is the quintessential Greek location. Fine sandy beaches rub shoulders with arid hills, and fertile valleys alternate with gorges full of tumbling waterfalls and fresh springs. The eye-catching villages are brimming with luxuriant vegetation amongst the good, solid, shipowners' houses built by mariners who grew rich sailing the seven seas. Andhros is a dream destination, especially as it has not (yet) been overrun by tourists. Besides being the home of shipbuilding families – the Goulandris, for instance, who financed the Museum of Modern Art at Hora, the island's capital – Andhros also supplied the Greek merchant marine with many sailors, officers in particular. The departure of these men, on voyages of two or three years, was the occasion of great excitement on the quayside at Gavrio, their port of embarkation. Tearful womenfolk waved their handkerchiefs, expecting never to see their men again ... As befits its seafaring tradition, Andhros boasts a Maritime Museum housing a wide collection of model boats and marine instruments. In the Archaeological Museum, also founded by the Goulandris, visitors can contemplate the famous *Hermes of Andhros*, a marble copy of the bronze original by Praxiteles.

KEA, SIFNOS AND IOS

Even in the Cyclades, those who love solitude and exotic surroundings will find they are spoiled for choice. Their initial target will be Kea, which has main-tained its own identity and is the first island on the sea route from Pireas. Bolder spirits will push on to Sifnos, in mid-Aegean, or Anafi, well to the east, a paradise for hikers who will adore its silence, its golden, sandy beaches and crystal-clear waters. Sifnos has been the birthplace of all of Greece's famous chefs, most of whom left to further their careers in Athens. The island also enjoys glorious scenery, tranquil little ports and some decent places to eat. If

If you want to appreciate the delights of Ios in summer, explore it in the early morning when the thousands of tourists, mainly young, are still in bed. There are some handsome patrician houses dating from the island's prosperity in the nineteenth century, as well as churches whose walls are regularly whitewashed by the villagers.

you want peace, avoid Ios: since the early 1980s, the island has been swamped by young Anglo-Saxon tourists who have imposed their way of life. During the summer, bars and discos never empty, pumping out thunderous music into the early hours. Fans of Homer hoping to visit the bard's tomb, in the north, are advised to make the journey in spring or autumn, when calm returns, especially as the island possesses numerous beaches accessible only to walkers.

*What resemble white cubes stacked
on the cliffs are typical Cycladean houses,
some bestriding the streets of the island's
capital. In centuries past, Ios, with its
well-concealed harbours, was a lair for
pirates. In ancient times it was covered
by oak forests whose wood was used for
boat-building, and it has maintained close
maritime links ever since.*

THE CATS OF THE GREEK ISLANDS

The Greek Islands, and in particular the Cyclades, are the kingdom of the cat. They are everywhere, most in fact being feral. They frolic in the sun, leap from roof to roof, terrace to terrace, never shy of slipping into restaurants and tavernas where the customers – tourists especially – are always happy to spare them a morsel of fish or meat. So common are these animals that they seem to be part of the landscape. They are a godsend to photographers: snapped against the white-washed stairways, in mid-leap against the azure skies or basking in the noonday sun, cats are the stars of Greece … Of all domestic animals, they are the only ones that can enter a church without provoking the wrath of the officiating priest: a sure sign of their acceptance by the locals …

THE ARGO-SARONIC ISLANDS

Lying so close to Athens that they are nicknamed the 'suburban isles', the five islands of the Saronic Gulf are a favourite refuge for Athenians escaping the capital. Many have a weekend retreat or even a second home here.

EGINA

Egina proudly claims to have been Greece's first capital in 1828. Before that, in classical times, it had enjoyed great prestige. The first Greek coinage, with its characteristic tortoise emblem, was struck on Egina in the sixth century BC. The island also possessed a powerful fleet, and did not hesitate, in 456 BC, to ally itself with the Persians to defeat its traditional rival, Athens. But the Athenians had the last word. After a nine-month siege, they inflicted a decisive defeat on Egina, whose citizens were deported and replaced by Athenian colonists. Still standing is a building dating from this period, one of the best preserved in Greece. Supported by stout Doric columns, the temple of Aphaia (the Invisible One), is to be found to the east of the island. Constructed from a yellowish local limestone, it was built in the fifth century BC on a prehistoric religious site. In its isolation on the summit of a hill and closely framed by a pine forest, it offers a splendid view over Egina and the sea below.

Amongst Egina's traditional activities, the main one is the cultivation of pistachio nuts, which have made a name for the island. The trees grow in the western region, where winds are gentlest, and produce some 20,000 tonnes of fruit per year. The local people also make fine glazed pottery, particularly the *Kanatia* or wide, two-handled water-jars associated with the locality since antiquity.

In classical times, the islands of the Saronic Gulf – here Egina – were originally colonies of Athens, before their growing power led to war with the mother city. Later they became the domains of shipowning families, the kapetanoi, *who were allowed by the Ottoman Turks to cruise the seas in their merchant vessels. During the War of Independence, they transformed these into a naval fleet and helped to harry the occupying power. Having amassed their treasures, they built superb fortified dwellings or* arhondika *to house them.*

POROS

Poros consists of not one but two islands: the pine-clad Kalavria, to the north, dominated by the hill of Vigla, and, to the south, the volcanic islet of Sfairia, whose principal town extends all the way along the busy strait. The islands' name derives from this quarter-mile-wide (400 m) strait (*poros*) separating it from Galatas, the premier village on the mainland coast of the Argolid. The tiled roofs and whitewashed houses of Poros Town, dominated by the clock tower, are bathed in pink at sunset. In the little port, there is a constant toing and

froing of caïques linking the island to Galatas. Visitors with an interest in history and archaeology – and a fondness for walking, as it is nearly 4 miles (6 km) to the site – will allow themselves to be enticed as far as the Temple of Poseidon with its remarkable panoramas. Though it is mainly in ruins, one cannot help thinking of Demosthenes, who poisoned himself here in 322 BC after being cornered by the agents of the Macedonians whom he had vigorously opposed for years.

The sanctuary of Apollo on Egina, known as the Kolona because of the sole column remaining upright. The temple was constructed in the fifth century BC and originally boasted 30 columns. Close by is a pretty beach surrounded by pines.

On the summit of a pine-clad hill overlooking the bay of Ayia Marina, the temple of Aphaia, on the island of Egina, is one of the best preserved in Greece. It displays similarities with that of Zeus at Olympia, built 30 years later in 460 BC. The superb sculptures from the pediments, representing combats of the heroes at Troy, are now in the Glyptothek (Museum of Sculpture), Munich.

IDHRA (HYDRA)

Once a pirate stronghold, Idhra can undoubtedly claim to have the finest port of all the Greek islands. It is surrounded by splendid houses dating from the 1700s, when such was its maritime supremacy that it gloried in the nickname of 'Little England'. The houses belonged to the great shipowning families like the Miaoulis, Koundouriotis, Tombazis and Boudouris families, who won fame on the high seas during the War of Independence, accumulating huge fortunes in the process. Some of these houses are now administrative buildings – the fine arts school or the officers' college, for instance – but others are open to the public, like the Koundoriotis dwelling with its museum devoted to the War of Independence. The island has no sandy beaches, but there are rocks from which you can dive to your heart's content into the clear, emerald waters. The countryside around Idhra Town is also great for walking, with the chance to discover isolated monasteries well away from the round-the-clock bustle of the port.

Idhra and its magnificent 'captain's houses', which have been meticulously restored. Quick travel between this and neighbouring islands is possible by hydrofoil or ferry. Sometimes so many boats operate simultaneously that there are traffic jams at sea! Vehicles are not permitted on Spetses, Poros and Idhra, thus assuring them of a certain tranquillity.

SPETSES

If possible, arrive on Spetses in the evening, just as the women are watering their gardens and filling the air with the soft fragrance of jasmine. Spetses has become home to some of Athens' most wealthy families, who have built luxurious villas here. With magnificent coves, delightful little beaches and pine forests, this is one of the best islands for relaxation. Take a horse-drawn cab, or, more prosaically, a bicycle, and explore the roads paved with marine-themed pebble mosaics like fish, seaweed or anchors and discover the old patrician houses and their stunning gardens packed with flowers. Sometimes you will need to grab the opportunity for a quick glance through the gates when they are opened, as most of these houses jealously guard their privacy behind high walls ... As in all spots on the tourist track, cafés and shops have mushroomed, while the ports, both the old and the new (Dapia), exhibit yachts and pleasure

craft swaying lazily in the breeze. Spetses shares with neighbouring Idhra the honour of having taken part in the War of Independence and given refuge to high-spirited heroines like Bouboulina, who defied the Turkish fleets. Her house, still in the hands of her descendants, is open to the public. To the extreme south you can make out the rugged little isle of Spetsopoula. It is privately owned by the Niarchos family, one of whose members is the shipowner famed as the rival to Onassis.

After the War of Independence, Idhra fell back into oblivion. It was only after the Second World War that it was rediscovered by foreign tourists, who have since made it one of Greece's most fashionable destinations. The accommodation there is to die for, and the island, which is car-free, is classified as a heritage site.

Three- or four-storey arhondika *line Idhra's port. They were built between 1780 and 1820 and now house state institutions that also undertake their maintenance. The sea front throbs with life from Easter to September as well as at weekends when Athenians abandon the capital for the pleasures of their own backyard islands.*

THE SPORADES

Four green islands stand guard off the promontory of Pilion in the western Aegean.
They are sometimes known as the Northern Sporades to distinguish them from the Dodecanese
or Southern Sporades. An abundant rainfall means they are wooded and covered with thick
vegetation, quite unlike the Cyclades. Their name means 'scattered islands'.

Skyros, the most eastern and distant of the Sporades, looks like a butterfly when viewed from the air. Thanks to its isolation in the midst of the Aegean, it has managed to preserve its cottage industries, being particularly known in the past for its furniture, especially its delicately worked tables and chairs, which were sold all over Greece. Many homes on the island still display old pottery, vividly painted plates or local embroidery woven with glowing colours. It is quite common to come across locals, particularly the older age group, wearing the traditional dress of shirt, embroidered jacket and baggy trousers. The Faltaïts museum houses a valuable collection of sculpted furniture and traditional costumes, including those used in carnivals. The capital, Skyros Town, takes longer to explore, requiring patience and endurance from the visitor on foot. Seen from a distance, it gives little clue to its labyrinth of tiny streets, the ever-narrowing steps leading up to the *kastro* and the cube-like houses seemingly jumbled in a heap. Now and again a gap between two of them allows a glimpse of the sea way down below. From on top of the fortress, the view is magical.

Skiathos, smallest of the Sporades, is prodigal in its welcome. Well-known members of the jet set find it the perfect place to spend a peaceful holiday incognito. Fine, sandy beaches fringed with pine trees – reputedly the best in the whole Aegean – lush woodlands of arbutus, poplars, chestnuts, lemons and olives, and some seventy little bays guarantee anonymity to those who desire it … and there's even an airport! Skiathos has accordingly become the most fashionable island of the archipelago. To the west, the extensive beach of Koukounaries, with its glorious setting, matches anything to be found in the Pacific. Swarms of holidaymakers invade the clear blue waters and golden beaches from the first warm days, harbours are full of spanking new – and often staggeringly big – yachts, while Germans and Brits imbibe the delights of this paradise on the café terraces. In summer, the island becomes a miniature Saint-Tropez with life definitely in the fast lane.

One wonders what Alexandros Papadiamantis would have made of all this frenzy; born here in 1851, a highly regarded writer of stories exploring the hardships of existence, his best-known titles are *The Murderess* and *Tales from*

Skyros, and its stacks of cliff-top houses. It was on this island that two heroes of antiquity, Achilles and Theseus, found refuge. The former was hidden, when a boy, in the court of King Lycomedes, disguised in girl's clothing, as his mother Thetis had received a prophecy that he would die in the Trojan war. When hostilities began, Calchas, priest and soothsayer of Apollo, declared that Troy could not be taken without the aid of Achilles. So Odysseus, pretending to be a merchant, was dispatched to Skyros, where he presented jewels and fine clothing to the women of the court. But amongst these items was a spear and a shield. Achilles snatched them up, and gave himself away …

a Greek Island. He pursued a career as a journalist in Athens, at the same time producing some 170 short stories and a number of novels all set against the backdrop of the islands. In 1908 he returned to Skiathos, where he died three years later. The house where he both came into the world and left it, charming and typical of the place in its simple comfort, can be found in the main street of Skiathos Town, the capital. It has been turned into a small public museum. When the pleasures of jetskiing, waterskiing and especially diving begin to pall, other attractions of a more spiritual nature still await the visitor. There are a number of monasteries, accessible on foot, that guarantee the chance to meditate and enjoy the entrancing views. Evangelistria is one such, dating from the 1700s; it stands above spectacular wooded gorges at a height of nearly 1,500 ft (450 m). Aficionados of ruins will press on to the *kastro* (fourteenth century) overlooking a peninsula on the north coast. Of the 300 houses and 22 chapels that made up this stronghold, only a few sad relics survive.

Whitewashed houses on Skyros, roofed with pink tiles that have gradually replaced slate; the wild and rugged setting conceals small, isolated beaches that remain unspoilt.

Skyros is also known for the 'Carnival of the Goats'. Young people disguised as old men (yeroi) don black capes and masks made of goatskin. They are joined by the nyphes – men disguised as brides. In the narrow streets of Skyros Town, the capital, yeroi and nyphes dance together to the tinkling of bells. The festival derives from the cult of Dionysos, god of wine and the grape.

Skopelos is the greenest of the Sporades. With its 360 churches, the monasteries of Mt Palouki, rising above the superb landscapes, and its lonely beaches, the island has unique charm. Though overshadowed by Skiathos, Skopelos bears no grudge; it has managed to preserve intact its original lifestyle – one that needs to be enjoyed before the tourist industry gets wind of its hidden treasures. Cradled in a bay that seems to have been designed expressly to fit it, Hora, the capital, is shaped like an amphitheatre and built into the hillside. It retains its fine traditional houses with their elegantly carved wooden balconies, their tiled or slated roofs, and miniature streets paved with pebbles and shells leading up to the Venetian *kastro*. On the southwest side, a pleasant village, Glossa, peers down over the little port of Loutraki. This is undoubtedly the best side of the island for sea views. Inland, there are flourishing ranks of fig, almond, olive and particularly plum trees; the plums of Skopelos are renowned throughout Greece, and when the phylloxera

virus decimated French vines in the 1940s, they were introduced to France as a replacement crop.

You will need to explore inland to enjoy the island, including the *kalivia*, centuries-old farmhouses huddling among the cypresses and olives. Some of these traditional structures are lived in all year round, others are used only during harvest or at the festivals of local saints. All possess outside ovens for drying the plums to make prunes, the island's chief product. Skopelos is not to be sneered at in culinary matters: there are some good restaurants, with exuberantly original menus.

To set foot on Alonissos, wildest and quietest of the Sporades, is to enter another world. The interior of this elongated island is characterised by hills alternating with valleys thick with olive groves. Aromatic plants like thyme and sage clothe the hillsides. Alonissos is also a sanctuary for birds like Cory's shearwater and Eleonora's falcon, which nest in inaccessible places, and also

The pleasures of swimming and lazing on beaches are matched by those of fishing; the locals practise the latter more or less all year round.

Audouin's gull, while its waters provide a haven for the Mediterranean monk seal (*Monachus monachus*). With only 250 specimens surviving in the Aegean, this seal is one of the world's most endangered species. To protect it, Greece's first maritime reserve was created here in 1992, taking in Alonissos and its seven satellites. Three hundred types of fish and dolphins live in the rich waters around Alonissos, as well as varieties of coral. In spring, migrating birds break their journey in the reserve. This determination to preserve its fauna and flora has allowed the little island to escape mass tourism – by no means the least of its blessings. But its history has been very difficult. In the distant past, Alonissos, like all the Sporades, was continually ravaged by pirates, particularly Barbarossa; then in the 1950s it saw its entire vine stock destroyed by disease. Finally, in 1965, an earth tremor seriously damaged the main town (Palea Alonissos), forcing the inhabitants to move down to the port of Patitiri, where ferries and hydrofoils now operate ceaseless relays in summer whisking tourists

Mention Skyros and you think of great beaches and magnificent landscapes. In the capital, you can also visit the Museum of Popular Art, opened in 1964 by Manos Faltaïts, the sociologist, painter, poet and peace activist. It is sited in an impressive house owned since 1870 by his family, and offers a comprehensive overview of the island's culture. There are displays of old books, regional furniture, porcelain plates and traditional costumes.

The slopes of the Sporades favour the cultivation of the olive, synonymous with Greece. The interior is well watered by streams and rivers, and has developed a small-scale system of agriculture which allows these islands to escape total dependence on tourism despite their harsh topography.

between the Sporades. There are even caïque taxis, shuttling from beach to beach and among the surrounding isles. The old capital, clinging to the summit of a cliff, is well worth the ascent. Virtually derelict for some thirty years after the quake, it is now taking on a new lease of life. The surviving houses have been restored by expat Germans and British, and traces of its old attractiveness have begun to re-emerge. From Palea Alonissos, those happy to proceed on foot will be spoiled for choice, with a variety of tracks inviting exploration. Be prepared to get lost, though, as there is still no map of the footpaths – but surely it will not be long before there is one ...

THE IONIAN ISLANDS

Very different from the traditional image of Greek islands, the Ionian group are more reminiscent of their close neighbour Italy. They are seven in number – Corfu (Kerkyra), Paxi, Lefkhada (or Lefkas), Ithaki, Kefallonia, Zakynthos and Kythira – lying like a string of pearls off Greece's eastern coastline. The islanders speak with a singsong accent and paint their houses in gentle pastel colours.

KERKYRA (CORFU)

The green island of Corfu, to the north of the archipelago, is the largest of the group. According to legend, it owes its name to the daughter of the river god Asopos, a nymph named Kerkyra (or Corcyra), with whom the philandering sea-god Poseidon fell in love. He brought her to the island, and the result of their union was Phaeax. All the Ionian isles, but Corfu in particular, have firm roots in myth, and were the setting for part of the story of Odysseus. In northwest Corfu, for instance, among the alternating coves and wooded promontories, is the beach where Nausicaa, daughter of the Phaeacian king, came across the hero sleeping. She escorted him back to the palace where her father Alcinous accorded him a courteous welcome and promised that the Phaeacians would help him regain his homeland. The hero joined in their games and feasting and went on to relate the tale of his adventures. Today, this coastal area is known as Paleokastritsa, an attraction for countless tourists who come to dive in its unusually clear waters.

If you want to savour the true atmosphere of Kerkyra, the capital, sit for a while enjoying a coffee on the Esplanade (Spianadha). Notice the belltower of St Spiridon, named after the island's most celebrated saint, and the fortress constructed by the Venetians to protect the port approaches. If you like museums, don't leave this magical, if oversubscribed, area without a glance inside the Museum of Asiatic Art – its collection is extra special – and the Byzantine Museum housed in an old church.

Corfu tends to be very crowded (the British and Germans adore it), and you will be threatened from all directions by ceaseless waves of scooters whose owners have only the scantest regard for the highway code. Yet Corfu still retains places accessible only to hikers, such as the beach at Myrtiotissa, wild and deserted. Other locations bring to mind famous writers who have fallen in love with the island. At Kalami, on the east coast, the young Lawrence Durrell penned a brilliant homage to the island and its people: *Prospero's Cell*. From Corfu you can take the hydrofoil to Paxi and Andipaxi; cars are forbidden on Andipaxi, so once the summer tourists have left, all is peace and quiet.

The old town of Corfu has an Italian flavour, with its tall, narrow apartment blocks linked by washing lines. The Ionians have also borrowed from Italy the graceful arcades that march alongside the squares on Corfu and Zakynthos. The fact is that the Venetians dominated these islands for more than four centuries before they fell under the sway of France – only briefly, but long enough for the French to plant trees of liberty on Zakynthos and Corfu and set up Jacobin clubs.

Italy or Greece, that is the question. People seem less solemn here, there is a sense of fun in the air, an inclination to indolence, especially on Corfu, but also a zest for life. The colours are different too. The pines are a crisp, bright green, the houses painted in shades of pink, ochre, light blue and orange, to which the roof tiles add an extra note of gaiety. Ionian islanders are great lovers of opera, painting and poetry.

Preceding double page:
Watching the sun set over Corfu is a unique
experience. The house-fronts are bathed in
a red, pink and orange glow; truly magical ...

A tiny island wholly occupied by a white
convent, Vlaherna lies south of Corfu Town;
it is a symbol of Corfu and is always being
photographed. The island is reached along
a causeway crawling with tourists in summer.
Opposite is Pondikonissi. or Mouse Island,
which is claimed to be the Phaeacian vessel
that carried Odysseus home and was turned
to stone by Poseidon ...

*North of Corfu, at Sidhari, Petaloudhes is a
geological curiosity: sandstone cliffs layered
like vanilla slices and incised with creeks,
tunnels and caves. The 'Canal d'Amour'
leading to the sea is a magnet for
holidaymakers, mainly Germans and British.*

LEFKHADA

Life moves at a different pace on Lefkhada. The scooters of Corfu are replaced by bicycles, and everyone seems the better for it. There are fine, empty beaches, and life retains a peasant quality that depends on the regularly recurring grape and olive harvests, so don't come here expecting a pulsating night life. What you will get are moments of relaxation in undisturbed natural surroundings, even if a few towns like Nydhri, Ayios Nikitas or Porto Katsiki are beginning to get very touristy. Lefkhada also possesses a musical tradition, which it strives hard to maintain.

ITHAKI

It was to Ithaki (classical Ithaca), where the long-suffering Penelope awaited him, that 'wily Odysseus' – the most famous hero, along with Heracles (Hercules), of Greek mythology – returned after his lengthy absence. According to Homer, Odysseus was king of the island, which was also his birthplace, but had left twenty years earlier to take part in the siege of Troy. Numerous places on the island still recall his adventures: there is the nymphs' grotto, where, at Athene's suggestion, he hid the gifts of the Phaeacians when he landed; Arethusa's spring; the plateau of Maratkia, supposed site of Eumaeus's hut ... and many more.

If it is peace and serenity you're after, spend a while on this wild and hilly island, and you're assured of sleeping soundly. The capital, Vathy, is a scenic little port tucked away in a bay lined with tavernas. The beaches mostly demand a few miles' walking, and most tourists depart again before nightfall, leaving Ithaki to its tranquillity.

Kioni on Ithaki is a first-class seaside resort wallowing in bougainvillea, jasmine – the scent when in flower is intoxicating – and laurel. There are frequent arrivals of cruise ships and the sheltered bay is fronted by restaurants and tavernas.

The traditional village of Kioni is swathed
in vegetation and lapped by waters shifting
between sapphire and emerald green.
The chic white houses all have similar
orange tiles, adding an extra note of gaiety
to the landscape.

Double page overleaf:
Legendary Ithaki with its deeply etched
coastlines that form a perimeter some
60 miles (100 km) in extent. The mid-section
is bitten out by the Gulf of Molos which
divides the island into two peninsulas
linked by a narrow tongue of land,
the Isthmus of Aetos. The highest point
is Mt Neritos, 2,600 ft (800 m).

KEFALLONIA

Whereas the eastern Aegean is dominated by the *meltemi* wind, the ruler of the Ionian coastline is the *maistro*, gusting among the islands to the delight of countless windsurfers. Many tourists have also taken up hang-gliding from the towering, white chalk cliffs like those at Myrtos, on Kefallonia, which boasts the best – or at least the most photographed – beach in Greece, with its ribbon of white sand against a backdrop of turquoise sea ...

Kefallonia is the sister isle of Ithaki, but its activities centre on the country-side, dotted with newly repainted houses with smart tiled roofs. The island produces a highly regarded wine (Robola). The chief town is Argostoli, somewhat noisy and worth visiting mainly for its Museum of History and Folklore, which illustrates varied aspects of island life. More attractive is the north, around Assos and its Venetian citadel, or Fiskardho, evocative of Saint-Tropez in the 1920s.

ZAKYNTHOS AND KYTHIRA

If you want to see seals and the loggerhead turtle (*Caretta caretta*), go to Zakynthos. In fact, the island is home to thousands of turtles that come to lay their eggs in the sand during the night. Unfortunately, the laying season is in August, which means these delightful creatures suffer a great deal of disturbance from the armies of tourists who invade the place in summer and crush large numbers of eggs. The northeastern beaches are particularly targeted by visitors and packed solid during the season.

Kythira, last and smallest of the Ionian isles, plays hard to get. Indeed, to reach it, you need to cross the entire Peloponnese, off whose southern coast it lies in splendid isolation. Here Aphrodite is said to have been born, and there are impressive gorges and remarkable grottoes, like that of Ayia Sofia. The scent of eucalyptus pervades the town of Hora; its stacks of houses nestle at the foot of a citadel and it enjoys lovely beaches, but they are attracting ever greater numbers of tourists.

A traditional image of a Greek Orthodox priest (papas) dressed entirely in black, with his long white beard and cylindrical black hat or skoufia. In Greece, churchmen are allowed to marry and have children when they are still deacons, that is, before their ordination. A priest's wife is called a papadia. Priests and their families mix freely with the local inhabitants and participate fully in community life.

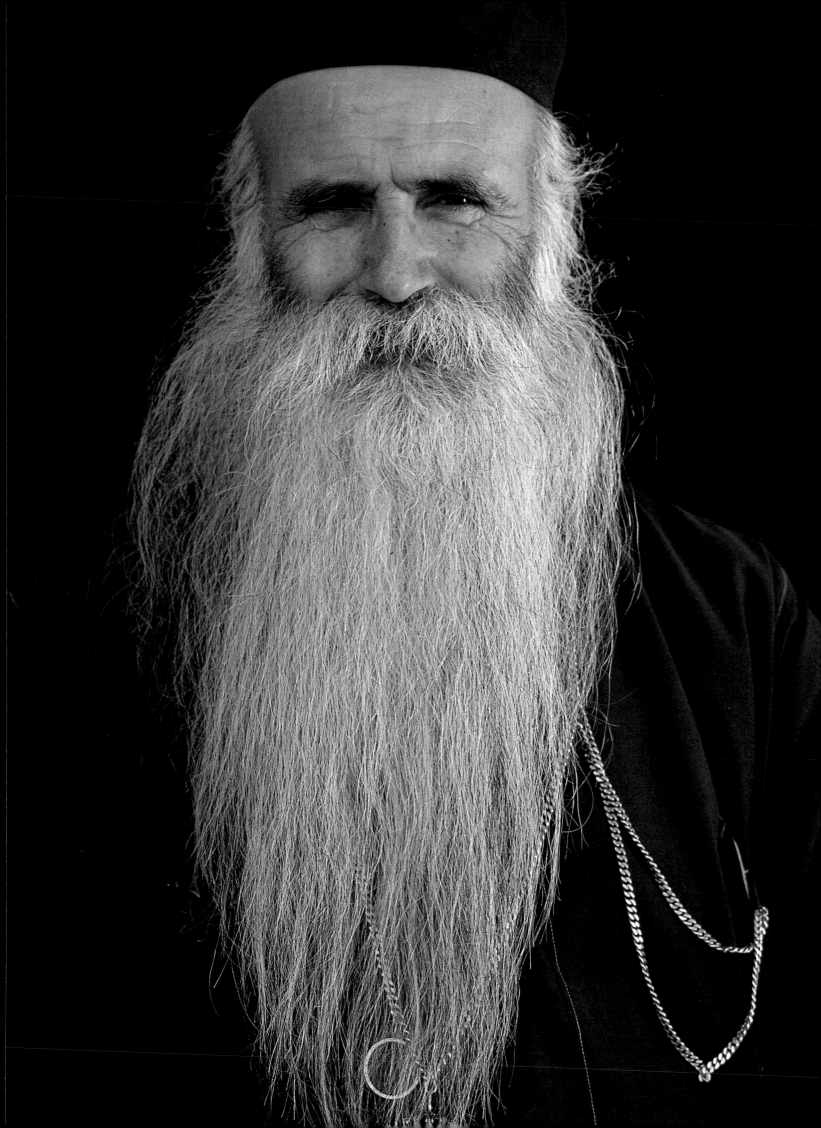

There are many monasteries on Kefallonia.
They will have been rebuilt several times
owing to the earthquakes that have
shaken the islands, notably that of 1953,
the most serious. The feast day of the
patron saint is the occasion for a festival,
attended by large crowds of visitors from
both Kefallonia and neighbouring islands.

The convent of Ayios Andhreas at Peratata consists of a seventeenth-century church – now a museum, and worth a detour, especially to see the frescoes – and a brand new building sheltering precious relics. The convent accommodates an order of cloistered nuns.

The katavothres *(small gulfs)* at the extremity
of the peninsula on which the capital, Argostoli,
stands are curiosities peculiar to Kefallonia.
They consist of fissures into which the sea
descends to re-emerge some 9 miles (14 km)
away around Sami and in the cave at Melissani.
The site of the fissures is marked by this
neoclassical rotunda.

Kefallonia is not all green valleys; there are arid peaks, particularly around Mt Ainos, situated in the national park of the same name. Wild horses now frequent what are the highest mountains of the Ionian islands, in classical times the site of a sanctuary dedicated to Zeus. The lower slopes provide pasture for sheep.

Preceding double page:
Greeks and tourists alike love to fish and dive
in the irresistible turquoise waters fringing the
Ionian coasts.

Low, drystone walls allow the islanders of
Zakynthos to cultivate terraces. In the interior,
home of the olive and the grape, they still
practise traditional agriculture. The coasts,
on the other hand, are the domain of tourism
and bursting with hotels and businesses: not
a happy outlook for the loggerhead turtles
whose habitat is the Ionian Sea.

On Zakynthos and Lefkhada, you come
across many women dressed in black:
widows who do farm work, their only
means of earning a living. The men's
tasks are to prune the olive trees and
harvest the ripe fruit – still done by
hand in these islands.

Hilly Zakynthos is bordered to the north by blindingly white cliffs rising sheer above the turquoise waters. There are boat trips to spectacular sites like Navaghio (also known as Shipwreck), where a vessel ran aground in the 1980s, or the Blue Grotto, with its extraordinary clear, turquoise and blue water.

THE CURIOUS PHENOMENON OF THE BLUE CAVES

The Ionian isles are very rich in marine caves to which boat excursions are available. On Kefallonia, in a cave where the limestone ceiling has collapsed, lies the subterranean lake of Melissani, with its astounding electric blue reflections. The lake came into being due to a curious phenomenon: the katavothres. These are fissures into which the water of the sea sinks, to re-emerge elsewhere, forming lakes of brackish water. When shafts of sunlight penetrate the opening in the cave roof, you will be privileged to witness a fantastical, kaleidoscopic spectacle of shifting hues and textures. Dhrogarati Cave, on the same island, has some impressive stalactites. The acoustics are so perfect that the place is used to stage concerts. On Zakynthos, the blue caves result from the action of sea on rock. The most celebrated example, the Blue Grotto, lies directly beneath the lighthouse on Cape Skinari. Discovered in 1897, it is famous for the extraordinary colour of the water, a blend of turquoise and deep blue, unparalleled in its transparency.

THE DODECANESE

In the extreme east of the Aegean, off the Turkish coast, stretches a string of twelve islands (Greek: *dhodekanisa*) which united in 1908 against the suppression by the Ottomans of privileges they had enjoyed since the sixteenth century.

RODHOS (RHODES)

The largest island of the archipelago, lying very close to the Turkish coast, is Rhodes, nicknamed for more than one reason the 'Island of the Sun'. As often in Greece, this epithet has its roots in antiquity. When Zeus, having become lord of the universe, divided up the Earth among the gods, he forgot Helios, who spent his time traversing the world from east to west. To repair his error, he presented him with the island. After all, Rhodes is reckoned to have 300 days' sunshine a year, which explains the incomparable luminous quality of its landscapes. The sun is of course vital for the growing of fruit – Rhodes is justly famed for its orchards – and flowers, which have earned the island another nickname: 'Isle of Roses'. The climate makes the many fine sandy beaches around its coastline a great attraction for tourists.

The name of Rhodes is, however, forever associated with the Colossus that was once its star attraction. This gigantic bronze statue, one of the Seven Wonders of the World and dedicated to Helios, stood, according to tradition, at the entrance to the port as a guide for ships in local waters and inspired the imagination of many an artist down the centuries. It was destroyed by an earth tremor in 225 BC and never rebuilt. Worse, when the Arabs invaded the island in 654 AD, its stones were sold off to a Syrian merchant, who needed 900 camels to cart them to their destination. Today, the site of the Colossus is marked by two columns surmounted by a stag and a doe.

The old town of Rhodes is a must for the visitor. To obtain your first, and unforgettable, impression, take a boat trip and discover it from the sea; a forest of towers, turrets and minarets soar above the city walls. Once in the town, avoid the restaurants galore posting menus in German and Scandinavian languages for the planeloads of tourists shuttling in and out all day, and seek out the narrow streets of the medieval town. It is encircled by massive ramparts, pierced with numerous gates and punctuated by high towers, an appearance it owes to the Knights of St John of Jerusalem, who made their headquarters here in 1309. They not only added the towers to the existing town, but also the Palace of the Grand Masters, a fortress where the population

The graceful profiles of a stag and a doe stand guard high above the port of Rhodes on the spot where, according to legend, the Colossus stood centuries before. The port serves as a link between the old town and the new. The locals meet up there in the evening for the volta, a traditional promenading ceremony during which they greet their acquaintances.

could take refuge in times of danger. The palace was destroyed in 1856 by the explosion of a powder magazine and reconstructed at enormous expense by the Italians in 1939–43 in the fourteenth-century style. The luxury of the building is reflected in its mosaic floors from the Roman and Early Christian periods, imported from Kos, the marbles of the central courtyard and the replicas of ancient statues. For two centuries the Knights resisted Ottoman assaults before succumbing in 1522 after a six-month siege by the armies of the sultan Suleyman the Magnificent. Some distance away, the Knights' Hospital includes a well-appointed Archaeological Museum; the *pièce de résistance* is the beautiful *Aphrodite of Rhodes*; the goddess is portrayed on one knee, holding up her hair to dry. But Rhodes has much more to offer. Worth investigating are the Byzantine Museum, The Folklore Collection with its vibrant homage to the island's traditions, and, for those interested in modern Greece, the Municipal Gallery exhibiting modern works of art; for the sports-minded, there is the golf

The medieval city of Rhodes, surrounded with moats and nearly 2 miles (3 km) of ramparts, consists of the Collachium – once the private preserve of the knights, and including the Street of the Knights and the Grand Masters' Palace – and the Lower Town where the rest of the population lived. The Archaeological Museum is housed in the former Knights' Hospital and the Byzantine Museum in a church that was the knights' cathedral before its transformation into a mosque.

course at Afandou, or horse-riding on the beach; and the amateur lepidopterist will make for Petaloudhes and the Valley of the Butterflies, a green and narrow vale where thousands of Jersey tiger moths are found between June and September, attracted by the scent of the *Liquidambar orientalis* trees, whose leaves are used for making incense.

But life exists outside Rhodes town and its environs – particularly at Lindos, reached after an hour's journey south along a good surfaced road. Architecturally, Lindos is a gem, with its whitewashed houses, its maze of tiny streets and its castle-cum-acropolis towering 300 ft (100 m) above the town. Here successive civilisations have built upon each other in a way resembling geological strata. It was occupied in 1100 BC by the Dorians, who with their commercial acumen established its future prosperity and founded colonies on the coasts of Asia Minor just across the water. Then came the Romans, followed by the Byzantines, to be replaced in their turn by the Knights of St John, who

erected the powerful fortress dominating the town – before the Ottoman Turks seized it from them. Later invaders were hippies – led by the rock band Pink Floyd – who discovered the delights of Lindos in the 1970s and decided to stay, placing it on the map once and for all. Now the town has become a magnet for the innumerable visitors who never tire of its beauty, and it's swamped by tourists in summer.

To the south of Rhodes, the baths known
as the Thermes Kallitheas were once
famous for their curative properties.
The domed pavilions, pink marble
columns and Moorish structures were
added by the Italians in 1929, when
they occupied the island. The baths are
now disused, but they and their pleasant
garden surroundings have served as sets
for several films.

SYMI

On the hillside overlooking the port of Symi is an array of pedimented neoclassical houses with elegant yellow, blue, ochre and wine-coloured facades. No less than 400 steps link the town to the port, Yialos, where several boats a day put in from Rhodes. In the nineteenth century, the island was known for its boatyards and sponge diving. Now, the former have fallen silent, though caïques are still made here, and the sponges come from Egypt, Florida or the coast of Cuba. But the people of Symi realised they still had a trump card to play: attracting tourists. They rolled up their sleeves and set to work repainting their beautiful but dilapidated houses in pastel shades, under the watchful eye of an archaeological commission charged with making sure the local style was respected. The gamble paid off. When you add to this scenario unspoilt beaches and numerous tracks to explore, Symi's future looks rosy. At the very south of the island, best reached by boat, the monastery of Taxiarchis Mihaïl Panormitis is a place of mass pilgrimage for Greek sailors on 8 November, the saint's feast day. The interior of the church, which contains a superb wooden baroque iconostasis, is crammed with thank offerings in the form of gold or silver ships.

KARPATHOS

Wild and rugged, Karpathos, to the west of Rhodes, was known in antiquity as Porphyris (from the Greek word meaning 'purple') because of the dye manufactured there. Later, it became the haunt of pirates. Today, although tourism has developed – the island boasts exceptional beaches like Ahata, Kyra Panayia and Apella on its east coast – Karpathos has managed to preserve its traditions, and the older inhabitants speak a dialect akin to the ancient Dorian language. At an altitude of nearly 2000 ft (600 m) and long isolated from the rest of the island, the village of Olympos still enjoys its ancestral way of life. The women continue to cook bread in communal ovens and wear traditional costume: brilliantly coloured skirt and apron, embroidered black sleeveless top

On Symi, Yialos, the port, is one of the most spectacular in Greece. It is linked to the town Horio, high up, by 400 steps. The whole is classified as a heritage site by the Greek Ministry of Culture, and no ugly building projects are permitted to interfere with the elegant array of neoclassical dwellings, which are regularly renovated.

and flowered scarf. On festival days, they don the necklace of gold coins –
always foreign currency (Ottoman coins, napoleons, dollars, English sovereigns),
which the mother of the family passes on to her eldest daughter on her
wedding day. In fact, social life is a sort of matriarchy, as on other islands of
the Dodecanese, like Leros. On Karpathos, the Easter festival involves even more
colourful ceremonies than in the rest of Greece, with icons, for instance, borne
in procession. This is part of the Orthodox rites scrupulously observed by the
islanders; but the national flag is carried at the head of the procession, as the
concepts of nationhood and religion are inseparable in Greece.

For a considerable time, Symi and other islands of the Dodecanese, like Kalymnos, practised sponge-diving in the Mediterranean. A small maritime museum relates the history of this activity, which was carried out by divers without breathing apparatus until the first compressed air suit appeared in 1865. Today the sponges sold on the island come from the coasts of Florida and Cuba.

KALYMNOS

Kalymnos was once celebrated for its sponge-diving. Until the 1970s, the inhabitants of this arid isle sailed the seas in search of sponges – the light and porous inner skeletons of multicellular marine animals – an industry they depended on for their livelihood. Each trip lasted six months; the fleet's departure in April or May and its return in September–October gave rise to high festivities in the port. Women and children thronged the quayside as the local Orthodox priest blessed sailors and boats. In-between times, the island belonged to the womenfolk. But nowadays the sponges sold here come from abroad.

The importance of tourism has increased in recent years, but Kalymnos still produces oregano, which makes a delicious seasoning for fish and Greek salads, a highly regarded thyme honey, and the mandarins and lemons grown in the beautiful Vathy valley on the east coast. The north of the island is crisscrossed with mountain tracks that make for pleasant hiking, surfaced roads being largely confined to the south. By now you will be not be surprised at the capital's white and blue houses; these are the national colours, and were a way for the inhabitants to display their intense attachment to their native Greece during the Italian occupation from 1912.

On Kalymnos, Miloi, with its three abandoned windmills, on the edge of the 'white town' of Horio (Hora). The latter was once the island's capital, but has now been replaced by Pothia somewhat to the south. Rocky and arid, supporting only meagre vegetation, Kalymnos nevertheless possesses one fertile valley, Vathy, where lemons and mandarins flourish.

KOS

Amateur archaeologists will be thrilled with Kos. For a start, it was the home of Hippocrates, father of modern medicine, which is no small recommendation. There is a lovely little square in the capital where stands what is claimed to be the great doctor's plane tree; it is enormous, with a girth of nearly 40 ft (12 m), but in reality it's 'only' 500 years old! Never mind, the tree is there, underlining how Hippocrates lived to the ripe old age of 100. Next to his tree is a handsome Turkish fountain. There is more. The island's history goes back to Neolithic times, but it achieved fame in the fourth century BC thanks to the Asclepion, the

great therapeutic centre of antiquity attended by patients from all over Greece. The complex stands 2½ miles (4 km) to the west of the capital amid eucalyptus trees, palms and cypresses on a grassy hill overlooking the sea. In the town itself many traces of antiquity survive. The agora contains Hellenistic ruins and very fine Roman mosaics; not far off, other mosaics have been discovered in the Casa Romana, a Pompeian-style villa, as well as baths, an odeum and a section of the Roman road. The Archaeological Museum houses some remarkable pieces, including a statue of Hippocrates. You may find all this culture rather overwhelming, so afterwards perhaps you should follow the example of the islanders by strolling round the port's pine- and jasmine-scented streets, and stopping somewhere for a glass of ouzo. Later you could head for Kefalos on the west coast with its magnificent sandy beach. Tourists, at least the younger ones, prefer to chill out on the beaches of Kardhamena (packed sardine-style) before hitting the nightclubs of this former fishing village.

Kalymnos also produces large quantities of water-melons. The Greeks eat fruit at all times of the day. The island, which boasts a history dating back to Neolithic times, is turning more and more towards tourism as its chief industry.

Kos: an islander taking it easy on the step of his dazzlingly white house. Whilst maintaining traditional agricultural activities such as fruit and vegetable growing, Kos has opened itself up to a large degree to international tourism, with planeloads of German and Scandinavian visitors jetting in during the season.

The Dodecanese also lay claim to some less well-known but interesting islands. Nissyros, according to legend, was once joined to its close neighbour Kos, before Poseidon tore it off and hurled it at the giant Polybotes during the violent war between the gods and the giants. Polybotes was buried under the present island and the volcano vents his anger on occasion. Rising nearly 2,300 ft (700 m) above the sea, it regularly produces smoking fumeroles; a pleasant hike will bring you to the top. Astypalea, to the far east of the island, near Amorgos, has a world's-end air about it, and recalls the Cyclades, with its windmills and its coastline indented by enticing little creeks.

PATMOS

To the northwest of the archipelago, Patmos is known as the isle of the Apocalypse, for it was here, in a grotto now referred to as the Sacred Cave, that St John the Evangelist wrote his prophetic Revelation, having been exiled by Rome from 95 to 97 AD. Maybe this is why Patmos is blessed with a unique spiritual aura. For the Greeks, this sacred isle is a major place of pilgrimage: the Easter processions are particularly well attended, as are those of 21 May, the saint's feast day. High above the white houses of the main town, Hora, the imposing monastery of St John the Evangelist (or 'Theologian', as Orthodox Greeks call him) was founded in his honour at the end of the eleventh century by Abbot Khristodhoulos 'the Blessed'. (The marble sarcophagus containing his remains is preserved in the Founder's Chapel.) There are frescoes here attributed to Cretan artists, particularly fine being those in the refectory depicting scenes from the life of Christ. The library houses over 3,000 ancient works and a thousand or so manuscripts, one of the largest Eastern collections. Below the grand old monastery nestles Hora, a tangle of whitewashed houses and flights of steps. It's a delight to lose yourself in the steep little streets where a welcome silence reigns among the oleanders.

But Patmos is more than a spiritual refuge. The island is fringed with fine sandy beaches, some of which must be reached by caïque. When the day-trippers disembark, it's fun watching them dashing here and there among the few trees trying to grab a spot of shade. They then spend the day swimming and lazing around before returning to Hora at dusk …

The monastery of Ayios Theologos on Patmos is one of the wealthiest and most influential in Greece. This popular place of pilgrimage massively dominates the main town; with its towers and buttresses it resembles a castle more than a monastery. The treasury is aptly named, housing over 200 icons, 300 silver items and jewels of enormous value.

The monastery of Ayios Theologos (St John
the Evangelist), on Patmos, is the scene of
major celebrations at Easter and on 21 May,
the saint's feast day. On Maundy Thursday,
hundreds of the faithful visit Hora to watch
the ceremony of the Washing of the Feet.
The abbot washes the feet of twelve monks,
in imitation of the actions of Christ, an act
of humility also practised by the Byzantine
emperors.

Because of their isolation from Athens, seat of central government, the Dodecanese were vulnerable and suffered successive invasions over the centuries, from the Knights of St John to Mussolini's Fascists. Among the invaders was Suleyman the Magnificent, who came in 1522. They were the last islands to be reincorporated into the Greek state, in 1948.

Double page overleaf:
Windmills are also found in the Dodecanese, but only those used as museums still function.

THE GREEK ORTHODOX EASTER: *KHRISTOS ANESTI*

The Greek Orthodox Easter is focused around three very special days. On the night of Good Friday everyone, candle in hand, takes to the streets to accompany the procession of the Epitafios: a wooden bier symbolic of Christ's Passion. On Holy Saturday evening, the bells ring out to mark the Resurrection. The faithful attend the Resurrection Mass in churches decked with flowers. At midnight, in total darkness, the priest lights his own candle; everyone then hurries to light his or hers from the sacred flame, thus transmitting the Light of the Resurrection from person to person, repeating: Khristos anesti ('Christ is risen!') as the bells sound overhead. Easter Sunday is devoted to the cooking and eating of the Paschal Lamb, emblem of Christ. Hard-boiled eggs, dyed red, are placed on the family table. The diners break their eggs, which are held in the right hand, against that of their neighbour, repeating: Khristos anesti. The neighbour replies: Alithos anesti! ('He is risen indeed!'). The feasting now begins, and will continue into the evening.

ISLANDS OF THE NORTHEAST AEGEAN

Along the Turkish coast is a series of islands with evocative names: the green isle of Thassos; Samothraki (Samothrace, famed for the *Winged Victory*); the volcanic landscapes of Limnos; Lesvos, homeland of the divine Sappho; Samos, renowned for its wine; and Hios, scene of the infamous Ottoman atrocities.

HIOS (CHIOS)

Hios was well known from the Middle Ages for its mastic, a resin used in liqueurs and a type of chewing gum; the Genoese, the occupying power at that time, built villages in the interior to protect the gum harvest. The *mastihohoria* are all laid out on the same pattern, with protective towers and houses grouped around a church. The people of Pyrgi, a very fine medieval town in the heart of the *mastihohoria* with narrow, partly covered streets, decorate the house walls with *xysta*: geometric designs cut into the whitewash to reveal a layer of black volcanic sand beneath. At the approaches to the capital, which is also the island's chief port, the fertile plain of Kampos is clothed with fruit trees. Close by, the seaside resort of Karfas offers a variety of beaches and coves. But Hios is also burdened with a sombre reputation; it was the scene of acts of genocide committed by the Ottomans in 1822 shortly after the outbreak of the War of Independence, when 25,000 inhabitants were slaughtered, with many others deported and their villages razed.

Perched way up on partly forested mountains some 6 miles (10 km) from Hios town, the monastery of Nea Moni, still in use, was founded in 1042 by the Byzantine emperor Constantine IX. A World Heritage Site since 1990, its eleventh-century mosaics with their gold backgrounds are amongst the finest in Greece. The dome was restored after the earth tremor which hit the island in 1881.

SAMOS

Samos is separated from the Turkish coast by a channel just over 1 mile (2 km) wide. Stony terraces provide a hold for vines and olive trees, jostling for position among the pine trees. The island was reintegrated into the Greek state only in 1912 after four centuries of Ottoman rule, punctuated by fierce struggles to cast off the apparently interminable yoke; now it has become a popular tourist destination.

The classical history of Samos is inseparable from the cult of Hera, wife of Zeus, to whom in the sixth century BC the inhabitants erected a temple, the largest in its day anywhere in Greece. The island then enjoyed stupendous development, dispatching its sailors and traders to every corner of the Mediterranean. From their lengthy odysseys they brought back many thank offerings which they consecrated in the goddess's temple. Not content with supremacy at sea, the

Samians revealed themselves to be formidable architects. Samos Town needed a water supply, and the only spring was on the other side of a hill. So a certain Eupalinos, a brilliant architect, decided to drive a conduit through the hillside beginning from each end simultaneously, just like the engineers on the Channel Tunnel. Ten years were required to excavate the 4,429 ft (1,350 m), and when the work parties met, it was exactly at the point calculated by Eupalinos! Samos was also the birthplace of the mathematician and philosopher Pythagoras, whose theorem is familiar to every child at school. So much for the glories of history, now for the delights of the palate ... Samos produces noted wines of the same name: a muscatel that serves as either an aperitif or dessert wine.

Though these islands are so close to Turkey, they enjoyed a golden age of Greek civilisation. Some of the brightest spirits of antiquity were born here, like Pythagoras and Sappho. But it takes time to get there: long boat journeys discourage many tourists, so that the islands remain relatively protected from the mass invasions suffered by some of their neighbours.

At the entrance to the monastery site, an ossuary contains the bones of numerous inhabitants of Hios who perished in the 1822 massacres, the subject of so much historical debate and the inspiration for the famous Delacroix painting. Many monasteries in Greece are still in use; behind their walls, men from another age devote themselves to the study of sacred texts.

Preceding double page:
At Pyrgi, on Hios, the inhabitants decorate
the outside of their houses with xysta.
Most are geometrical designs, but flowers,
leaves or animals are also found. The technique
consists of lining the walls with a mixture of
cement and volcanic sand and adding a layer
of whitewash. Patterns are then scratched into
the surface, revealing the grey base.

The beach at Emborios, in the very south of
Hios, is covered with black pebbles. In the
surrounding area, rich archaeological finds
have been made by the British School at
Athens. The site was first inhabited in the
Bronze Age, and was successively home to
an archaic temple, a classical building, and
an Early Christian basilica.

*Inhabited since ancient times, Hios town
is dominated by the minareted mosque and
the* kastro *or fortress commanding the port
entrance. Under the Genoese, Hios was a
busy city controlling the highly lucrative
mastic trade. In 1566 the island fell to the
Ottomans; it failed several times to throw
off their yoke and was not finally reintegrated
into the Greek state until 1912.*

*Double page overleaf:
Hios. The sea with its oil-like sheen laps a
ruined tower. Fishing remains a traditional and
lucrative activity highly prized by the Greeks.*

LIMNOS, SAMOTHRAKI AND THASSOS

Limnos is well worth exploring, as it still has a number of totally unspoilt areas. The tourists dig in around the chief town, Myrina, and the long beaches of fine sand are quite deserted. In classical myth, Limnos, like neighbouring Samothraki (Samothrace), was a favourite haunt of the Cabiri, divinities of farm and countryside associated with fertility. On Samothraki you can find evidenc of their cult in the Sanctuary of the Great Gods, one of the finest – and most peaceful – sites in the whole Aegean. It was also on Samothraki where the majestic *Winged Victory* marble statue was discovered; it now occupies a place of honour in the Louvre in Paris.

Not far off the coast of Thrace lies Thassos, a green island clothed with pines which was a place of great prosperity in ancient times. If you are an archaeology fan, you will be thrilled by the remains to be found there; but, having investigated the past, don't miss out on the unspoilt beaches.

LESVOS

If you had to choose a single island, it ought to be Lesvos. Known in classical times as Lesbos, it was the inspiration for poets, philosophers and musicians and was the home of Sappho, famous for her lyric verse. Nicknamed the 'Garden of the Empire' by the Ottomans, the island has always been extremely fertile, with numerous valleys devoted to growing grapes and particularly olives. Since antiquity the sulphurous hot springs around Therma have been sought out for their curative properties, and there are some magnificent beaches, including Mithymna in the north and Skala Eressou. Tourists love the fascinating landscape from the mountain villages to the little coastal resorts with their harbours.

Lesvos. The sixteenth-century monastery of Limonos was founded by St Ignatius: visitors can still see his cell. In the central church there is a fine sculpted wooden ceiling, notable arcading and a spring of holy water. The monastery also houses some outstanding icons, ancient manuscripts and religious jewellery.

Ὁ ἅγιος ἸΣΙΔΩΡΟΣ ἐν Χίῳ · Ὁ ἅγιος ΑΝΔΡΕΑΣ ὁ στρατηλάτης ὁ Πέρσης · Ὁ ἅγιος ΙΑΚ...

*Grouped in the east of Lesvos are the islands'
two main seaside resorts and some welcoming
spas. Large numbers of visitors also come
for the region's other attractions, including
delightful little ports like Plomari (the
'ouzo capital' with its five distilleries) or
Molyvos, the most picturesque, with its
superb noblemen's houses (*arhondika*)
arrayed beneath the* kastro.

*Double page overleaf:
Modern Mytilini town, capital of Lesvos,
occupies the same site as ancient Mytilene.
It is a bustling place with a particularly lively
market. The 450-year Ottoman occupation
has left its traces on the hillside terraces of
fine houses overlooked by the squat, rounded
domes of Ayios Therapon and Ayios Theodhoros.*

Reading the newspapers is a special activity
for Greeks, who have a passionate relationship
with the press. There are over 100 national
dailies, not to mention local papers, like this
one in Mytilini town. A favourite place for
reading the news and exchanging reactions
is the kafenio (coffee house). In addition to the
dailies there are numerous weekly or monthly
political reviews.

Opposite:
Donkeys, mules and goats are man's best
friends on the Greek Islands, well-suited to the
pace of life there.

*The interior of Lesvos is both breathtaking
and austere, its pine forest alternating with
olive groves. The olive is one of the island's
great treasures and there are reckoned to be
some eleven million trees. Odysseas Elytis
lived for many years on Lesvos, his ancestral
home, and the olive features throughout his
verse: 'Innumerable olive trees / Whose arms
will sift the light / Until, impalpable, it drifts
like snow in your sleep.'*

Midway between East and West, Lesvos, largest of the Greek Islands after Crete, is dotted with hundreds of tiny, hamlets (every house whitewashed) and small country villages where pastel shades predominate. A network of mule paths links the various communities.
Away from the coasts, a pastoral way of life still prevails, as is clear from the large flocks of sheep.

THE OLIVE – AS OLD AS TIME

Though Lesvos is the home of the olive, the tree, so much associated with Greece, is found throughout the country. Its squat profile is immediately recognisable, together with its distinctive grey-green leaves, and forms an essential element of the Greek landscape. It has managed to adapt perfectly to the poor, arid conditions, demanding only one thing from Nature: a temperature above 46.4°F (8°C). The time of harvesting depends on the type of oil required; some fruits are picked in autumn when green, others when black in late winter or early spring. On some islands, due to a lack of resources, the fruits are beaten down with sticks, or manually plucked or shaken from the tree, but wealthy growers use machines. With all these methods, vast nets are spread to catch the fruit. The Greeks are the world's largest consumers of olive oil, at 35 pints (20 litres) per head per year!

CRETE

Crete is the largest of the Greek Islands, almost a country in itself rather than an island. It boasts a wealth of resources in its 3,200 sq miles (8,300 km²) of coast, mountains, plains and caves, not to mention 500,000 inhabitants.

Crete is a wild place, with a long chain of mountains regarded throughout history as unassailable strongholds, topped by Mt Ida (over 8,000 ft/2,456 m) and separated by dizzying chasms cut into the rock. The beaches are vast and suit all tastes – golden sand or black pebbles – while the caves are counted in hundreds. And there is a wind that never ceases blowing. Lying between three continents – Africa, Asia, Europe – the island has aroused the envy of a string of conquerors. But the fierce spirit of the Cretans and their passion for freedom has allowed them to hold their own against successive invaders. Sometimes this resistance has cost them dear. They were forced to fight the Venetians from 1204, then the Ottomans, who took 21 years to capture the island – or rather the lowlands, as the mountains proved impossible to subdue. The Ottomans remained until 1913, and then World War Two brought the Nazis.

No mention of Crete would be complete without some tribute to the glories of the Minoan culture that emerged here around 2,000 years BC, making it one of the oldest in the Mediterranean basin. This mysterious civilisation was brutally destroyed around 1450 BC by a gigantic tidal wave arising from the eruption of Thira, the volcano on Santorini. But countless works of art have survived, including frescoes revealing remarkable artistic talent. It was an English archaeologist, Sir Arthur Evans, who first excavated the ruins of the Palace of Knossos, the largest in Crete. Constructed for King Minos, it consisted of no less than 1,300 rooms.

Most travellers visiting Crete (2.5 million each year) do so to see Knossos, but with a secondary interest in the island's many natural beauties. The climate is one of the most temperate in Europe, especially on the southern coast. You can swim in the sea from April until October, sometimes longer ... And the coastline offers contrasting attractions. To the extreme northeast, around Vaï, Kitropatia and Ayios Nikolaos, or to the west (Falasarna, Elafonisi), tourists are met with the sight of immense, managed beaches complete with parasols, sunbeds, snackbars and tavernas galore. The beach at Vaï is even fringed by a legally protected grove of rare palms. On the other hand, to reach the immense,

At Hania, the old quarters huddle round the thirteenth-century port dominated by Fort Firkas; once the residence of the Venetian governor before being transformed into a barracks and then a prison, it is now home to the Naval Museum. Not far off, the lighthouse (right) in minaret form at the end of the mole recalls the Ottoman occupation.

virtually deserted expanses of beach at Kommos, near Matala in the south, or Kissamos and Xerokambos in the west, you need to either borrow a boat or undertake a long trek on foot. But it's well worth the effort; the landscapes are totally different, and you feel you have ended up in some lost region of Africa or the Near East.

There's plenty for hikers, too. The best-known areas are the gorge at Samaria in the southwest, a magnet for thousands of ramblers every year, but the Valley of the Dead (eastern Crete) and the gorge at Therissos (below the White Mountains, Lefka Ori, south of Hania) are just as spectacular. The Samarian Gorge, declared a national park in 1962, is Europe's longest, extending over 11 miles (18 km). The walls are 2,000 ft (600 m) high and the narrowest point, the Iron Gates, is only 10 ft (3 m) wide. The place is the domain of eagles, falcons, buzzards and vultures, as well as the *kri-kri* or Cretan ibex. Should you prefer potholing, you are definitely in luck: Crete has some 3,000 caves, many of

A few miles from Iraklion, the ruins of the Palace of Knossos reflect the wonders of the Minoan civilisation. The restoration was begun in 1906 by Sir Arthur Evans, who took many liberties with the style, painting the walls and columns in supposedly Minoan colours. The palace occupies an area of 140,000 sq ft (13,000 km²) and is Crete's most visited monument.

At Knossos, more than 1,300 rooms were linked by corridors, stairways and deep, narrow light-wells forming a multistoreyed labyrinth. The frescoes included scenes of bullfighting, processions of young men and maidens carrying libation vases in honour of King Minos, dolphins and exotic birds.

which were inhabited in Palaeolithic times and after, with some serving as religious centres.

The towns are just as rich in interest. Iraklion, noisy and over-busy, hardly merits a lengthy stay but it's worth paying a visit to the walled Venetian quarter and also the Archaeological Museum. This has an important and unique collection of Minoan art treasures discovered on the island, notably from the palace of Knossos. After this, head for Rethymnon and Hania, lapped by a turquoise sea and enjoying sunsets that bathe the quayside houses in golden reflections. Rethymnon was an intellectual centre for centuries, and stands on the site of an ancient Minoan city. It possesses a provincial charm that entices you to wander around in a smug state of contentedness and succumb to the very Oriental indolence of the port, which has retained some handsome Italian-style loggias and several small palazzi. The old quarter also bristles with structures inherited from the four centuries of Venetian occupation, notably

the Rimondi Fountain, the Fortezza – a powerful fortress commanding the approaches, scene every year of concerts and a theatre festival dedicated to the Middle Ages – and the *Megali Porta* (Great Gate), the only surviving trace of the old city wall. The sea front is lined with cafés usually crowded with tourists. Make a point of diving into the area behind the port and exploring the narrow streets; you pass between rows of houses with wooden fronts and corbels dating back to Ottoman times. The Turks have left other traces in the slender minarets of numerous mosques: peeping over the rooftops. The Nerandzes Mosque (seventeenth century) is one of the best preserved. And if you want a glimpse of the traditional Crete, don't miss the little Historical and Folk Art Museum. Every form of local craft is represented there, in particular the superb embroidery work, lace, jewellery and furniture.

Hania has even more appeal, and has lost little by being replaced in 1971 by Iraklion as the island's capital. The scars of the last war have healed over –

The Preveli monastery stands huddled against the rock face on a spellbinding, desolate site overlooking the sea. It is still inhabited. The huge central court is enclosed by a nineteenth- century church and a small museum displaying liturgical objects.

Preceding double page: The sea-front at Rethymnon, with its glowing colours and fishing boats, is the town's nerve centre. A shame the cafés have lost their local flavour.

Crete is an island of mountains. The highest peak is Mt Ida (8,000 ft/2,456 m), in mythology the site of the birth of Zeus, king of the gods. Rhea, his mother, concealed the infant in a cave to thwart the attempts of Cronos to devour him.

German paratroops seized the airport at Maleme in 1941 – and the city long ago won over its quota of tourists. To make the most of its attractions, start the day at the port with a coffee or a honey yoghurt – and end it with plate of *mezes* (starters) washed down with ouzo.

Vestiges of the Venetian occupation are everywhere here: houses with paved inner courtyards, finely carved wooden balconies, and stone entrances crowned by pediments ornate with family crests and sculpted mottoes. On the quay, the bastion of San Salvatore recalls the power of the Serenissima in the days when she unhesitatingly sent her most brilliant engineer, Sanmichele, to this and other Cretan towns to build fortifications. The sixteenth-century arsenals could hold up to 40 galleys.

Behind the port, the little streets wind here and there under arches or vaulted passages beneath the loggias. In the old town, in the Spiantza quarter, you can step along the fine paved streets and admire Turkish dwellings with their wooden corbelling. The Archaeological Museum, housed in the former fifteenth-century church of St Francis (now completely restored), has displays of Minoan pottery, painted sarcophagi and third-century mosaics unearthed in Hania. In the gardens, a splendid Ottoman fountain rubs shoulders with a Venetian gateway, a microcosmic résumé of the city's history. And Crete would not be Crete without its markets hawking their prodigious array of wares; the one in Hania is typical, built in 1913 on the site of a former souk. Cans of olive oil jostle with leather sandals, watermelons vie for space with the decorated salt-paste crowns that are handed out at weddings to bring good luck. As if this wasn't enough, Hania possesses the ultimate luxury for a city: a series of beaches strung out along 12½ miles (20 km) of the coast to the west.

And then there are the mountains. The interior is replete with treasures, notably the monasteries perched eyrie-like on awe-inspiring and desolate sites. From Rethymnon, a tortuous road snakes among the gorge of Kourtaliotiko to the monastery of Moni Preveli, consisting of two groups of buildings of which only the Pisso Monastiri (Rear Monastery) is still intact and inhabited. This sanctuary was a regular centre of resistance against the Ottomans, who, by way of reprisal, did not hesitate to wreck much of it. The church was rebuilt in 1836, and contains some fine icons, including a Virgin portrayed as the Source of Life and a silver and gold reliquary cross. Another equally scenic route leads to Moni Arkadhi, ultimate symbol of the Cretans' passion for liberty. There, amid spectacular scenery, stands a monastery that was the site of violent clashes between the local peasants and the occupying forces during the 1866 rebellion. Though the building contained hundreds of refugees, Abbot Gabriel preferred to ignite the powder magazine rather than surrender. The slaughter – of Turks and Greeks alike – was horrendous, and there was only a single survivor, a young woman. Unsurprisingly, Moni Arkadhi is a place that still cruelly haunts Crete's collective memory. The buildings are eighteenth-century, except the church (late 1500s). The latter suffered little in the wars – there is a sumptuous

Precipitous cliffs near Anopoli, where a track leads as far as Aradena on its plateau 1,970 ft (600 m) above sea-level and overhanging the gorges. Four miles or so (7 km) further on, 2,300 ft (700 m) up and at the end of the world, is marooned the village of Ayios Ioannis. It is buried among the olive groves at the foot of the Lefka Ori *(White Mountains), its few houses terraced on slopes among scattered pines and cypresses.*

double nave and the Venetian portal (1587) is a harmonious arrangement of twinned Corinthian columns, pilasters and classical arches.

Among these mountain villages you may well bump into old, proud-looking Cretans wearing the traditional black headscarf or *mandili*. Their eyes are usually pale in colour, their faces sculpted by time and the weather, magnificent examples of a people with an indomitable will not to yield. One of the island's greatest standard-bearers was author Nikos Kazantzakis, born in 1883 at Candia, now Iraklion, with *Zorba the Greek* and especially *Freedom or Death* presenting a vast fresco of his native isle.

The interior of Crete is dotted with small churches and chapels, often cared for by private individuals anxious to see traditions maintained. The months pass to the rhythm of innumerable religious festivals. How many monasteries there are is uncertain; some, in the remote wilderness, radiate a spiritual atmosphere that invites contemplation.

Surrounded by mountains, the Lasithi plateau (around 2,800 ft/850 m above sea level) is a vast, fertile area producing mainly apples and potatoes. Hundreds of wind pumps used for irrigation used to lend the region a romantic atmosphere. Today they have been replaced by somewhat more prosaic diesel engines ...

MEN IN BLACK

Cretans have remained very faithful to tradition and even today the men, particularly the older age group, continue to wear local costume. You meet them on their doorsteps, in the streets or chatting in the café, heads wrapped in the mandili, a black scarf with fringes falling onto the forehead. They also wear the vraka – baggy knee-length trousers – and high black-leather boots. A shirt and waistcoat are worn beneath their jacket – also black. Black perhaps represents the grief they felt over their lack of freedom, for which they had to wait for centuries. On feast days they tuck a silver dagger called a bassalis in their belts, which consist of a length of material of 25 ft (8 m) or more wrapped around the waist. Their love of arms is an ancient affair, dating back to earliest antiquity, the time of King Minos and his palace at Knossos …

GREECE AT A GLANCE

Greece lies on the eastern borders of Europe and is bounded by the Ionian Sea to the west, the Sea of Crete to the south, and the Aegean to the north. It shares land frontiers with Albania, Macedonia, Bulgaria and Turkey. Eighty per cent of the country consists of mountain chains, including the Rhodope in the northeast, Pindus in the west (the largest), Parnon in the Peloponnese and the White Mountains in Crete. The highest peaks on the mainland are Olympus (9,570 ft/2,917 m), Giona (8,235 ft/2,510 m), Parnassus (8,061 ft/2,457 m) and on Crete, Mt Ida (8,058 ft/2,456 m). With a surface area of 50,969 sq miles (132,000 km²), Greece is a maritime nation, and no point is more than 55 miles (90 km) from the coast. The distance between London and Athens is around 2,000 miles (3,000 km).

Population: **10,939,000**
Capital: **Athens, 800,000; 3,000,000 inc. suburbs**
Head of State: **Konstantinos Stefanopoulos, 1995–**
Highest point: **Mt Olympus (9,570 ft/2,917 m)**
Official language: **Modern Greek**

FORMALITIES

Documents
UK passport allows you to stay up to three months, after which a visa extension is required. To hire a car you will need to produce an international credit card and a UK driving licence.

Custom
International regulations in force. The export of antiques is forbidden.

Useful addresses
Greek Tourist Office: 4 Conduit Street, London W1R 0DJ. Tel: 020 7734 5997.
Greek Embassy: 1A Holland Park, London W11 3TP. Tel: 020 7229 3850
Go Greece (www.gogreece.com); Ellada –Greece (www.ellada.com);
Matt Barrett's Greece Travel Guide (www.GreekTravel.com);
Greece Travel Guide (www.leisureplanet.com)

WHEN TO GO

Temperature
The summer months (July–August) are often very hot, with temperatures reaching 104°F (40°C) or more, without a drop of rain. May–June and September–October are the best periods.

Climate
There are far fewer tourists in May–June and September–October and the temperatures are quite pleasant, averaging around 82°F (28°C) by day and 59–68°F (15–20°C) at nights. The *meltemi*, a northerly wind blowing over the Mediterranean, can be quite strong in summer.

Local time
GMT +2; when it's British Summer Time (BST), Greek time is only 1 hour ahead of London.

Clothing
You need to pack comfortable shoes and, for summer, light cotton clothing, a pullover for boat crossings out of season, and warmer outfits for winter. Women need a skirt, not trousers or shorts, if they want to visit the monasteries, and also a garment that covers the arms.

Travel on/between islands
Ferries: see the Internet site www.gtp.gr for inter-island services.
By air: Olympic Airways operates numerous links between Athens (or Thessaloniki) and the islands, and also inter-island flights.
Buses: Frequent services link towns and villages on the islands.

CURRENCY

Exchange
Greece, in common with most other European Union countries, has now adopted the euro as its currency. Banks, savings banks and bureaux de change will exchange foreign currency and traveller's cheques. Cash machines accepting Visa, Mastercard and American Express cards are available in most towns.

Budget
The introduction of the euro has sent prices soaring in Greece. Hotel rooms, in particular, have gone up dramatically, as has the price of breakfast in hotels, regularly €10 nowadays. Even if you stay in private accommodation, it's not uncommon to be charged €60 just for a room. Restaurants are cheaper than in London, and you can eat well for €12.

Tipping
It's usual to leave a tip of around 10% in restaurants and give something to hotel porters.

ACCOMMODATION

There is a well-developed hotel infrastructure on the islands, especially those specialising in tourism. All categories are represented. You can also find accommodation in a private house. It's wise to book up many weeks in advance at the popular resorts if visiting in the main holiday season.

All telephone codes below and overleaf should be preceded by 0030

The Cyclades
Amorgos: Hotel Egialis (tel: 22 85 07 33 93) at Eyiali: plush, overlooks bay of same name. Milos: Kapetan Georgantas, in centre of Adhamas (Adamas) (tel: 22 87 02 32 15), en route to Plaka: air-conditioned rooms, pool. On Mykonos you're spoilt for choice: among the best are the Mykonian Ambassador (tel: 22 89 02 42 33) at Platys Yialos, the island's most luxurious hotel, all rooms with sea view; and at Ornos the Kivotos Club, offering superior levels of comfort (tel: 22 89 02 57 95). Paros: Hotel Petres at Naoussa (tel: 22 84 05 24 67), traditional Cycladean style; Hotel Astir of Paros (tel: 22 84 05 19 76), luxury category, with bungalows recalling a Greek village. Santorini: in Fira, the Kavalari (tel: 22 86 02 24 55) clinging to a cliff face, with rooms overlooking the caldera; cave-houses to let – apply at hotel. Syros: at Galissas the Dolphin Bay (tel: 22 81 04 29 24) is on the beach but with bungalows at various levels on the hillside; at Finikas (tel: 22 81 04 30 10) the Kokkina Beach offers superb sea views.

The Argo-Saronic Islands
Egina: Eginitiko Arhontiko, entirely renovated mansion, sumptuous décor, the island's no. 1 privately owned quality hotel (tel: 22 97 02 49 68). Idhra: Hotel Bratsera, former sponge factory, totally renovated but retaining charming original atmosphere and memorabilia, refined décor (tel: 22 98 05 39 71). Spetses: Nissia residence, luxuriously appointed in local style (tel: 22 98 07 50 00).

Ionian Islands

Kefallonia: At Sami, Hotel Pericles (tel: 26 74 02 27 80), amid woodland. Corfu: Hotel Kavalieri, plushest in the old town, with superb Anglo-Venetian décor (tel: 26 61 03 92 83). Kythira: Filoxenia (tel: 27 36 03 31 00), excellent hotel very near the sea. Ithaki: Hotel Kapetan Yiannis (tel: 26 74 03 31 73), bright, white-painted rooms overlooking port of Vathy. Lefkhada (Lefkada): Odyssey Hotel at Ayios Nikitas (tel: 26 45 09 73 51), garden setting with flowers and lawns, near the sea.

The Sporades

Skiathos: Skiathos Princess (tel: 24 27 04 92 26), on the beach at Ayia (Aghia) Paraskevi; luxurious, with two pools. Skopelos: Hotel Elli (tel: 24 24 02 29 43), prestigious, privately owned. Skyros: Skyros Palace: (tel: 22 22 09 19 94), largest on island, very near Girimasta beach.

The Dodecanese

On Kos, the Aeolos Beach at Nea Alikarnassos, excellent beachside accommodation (tel: 22 42 02 67 81). Patmos: Delfini, at Skala, very pleasant rooms and patio overlooking garden. Rhodes: Marco Polo Mansion, *the* place to stay (tel: 22 41 02 55 62), historic Turkish baths, period furniture and carpets.

Islands of the northeast Aegean

Hios: Chandris (tel: 22 71 04 44 01), international class hotel. Limnos: Porto Myrina Palace (tel: 22 54 02 48 05), every comfort, built on exact site of Temple of Artemis (foundations visible). Mytilini: Hotel Olive Press at Molyvos (tel: 22 53 07 12 05), former olive oil factory, stone's throw from the sea. Laureate, in Mytilini (tel: 22 51 04 31 11), renovated 1880s mansion. Samos: at Klima, the St Nicholas (tel: 22 73 02 52 30), de luxe accommodation, on Mikali Square.

Crete

Hania: Casa Delfino (tel: 28 21 09 30 98), luxury suites in former Venetian palazzo. Ayios Nikolaos: Minos Beach (tel: 28 41 02 25 48), private beach, set in landscaped gardens dotted with whitewashed bungalows. Iraklion: Galaxy (tel: 28 10 23 88 12), built round the pool and patio. Rethymnon: we recommend the Fortezza (tel: 28 31 02 38 28).

FOOD

Basic Greek fare consists of meat (lamb, pork) or fish, accompanied by plenty of olive oil, tomatoes and cucumbers; speciality Mediterranean vegetables such as aubergines and peppers also figure in abundance.

The Cyclades

Amorgos: at Eyiali, for a beautifully prepared meal, the Taverna Nikos. Milos: Pendema, on a terrace overlooking the port, Greek specialities. Mykonos: The Archeon Gefsis (brilliant décor) does re-creations of Ancient Greek dishes. Paros: the Levendi, with Oriental specialities served in a vine-covered courtyard. Santorini (Fira): Koukoumarlos, gourmet cooking and original menu with island wines. Syros: Lily's Taverna at Ermoupoli is one of the island's best-known eateries with popular music at weekends.

The Argo-Saronic Islands

Egina: Ippokambos, the best *mezes* (hors-d'oeuvre) on the island. Idhra: The Garden specialises in spit-roasts. Poros: Taverna Karavolos. Spetses: Taverna Patralis; its fresh fish and seafood are fantastic.

The Ionian Islands

Kefallonia: The Captain's Table, at Argostoli, has spiny lobster as its *pièce de résistance*. Corfu: The Venetian Well, on the island's finest terrace above an idyllic square. Kythira: Taverna Panaretos, traditional cuisine. Zakynthos: Taverna Anekia, thoughtful taverna menu; you eat to the sound of traditional music.

The Sporades

Skiathos: The Windmill, first-class menu and the staff speak English. Skyros: the Filippeos at Linaria – for lobster fans.

The Dodecanese

Kos: Psaropoula, a taverna excelling in fish dishes. Kalymnos: Taverna Argos, outstanding local cuisine. Karpathos: Xefteris, outstanding taverna, fish- and lamb-based menu. Patmos: Grigoris Grill, for fish grills. Rhodes: Fotis restaurant, fish and seafood . Symi: the Tholos, high quality.

Islands of the northeast Aegean

Hios: Bel Air, very chic. Limnos: Filoktitis, at Myrina, authentic cuisine and probably the best on the island. Lesvos: at Plomari, the Amoudeli serves fish grilled over a wood fire.

Crete

Hania: O Anemos, great choice of shellfish, occupies old Venetian mansion. Iraklion: Loukoulos restaurant, romantic ambience. Rethymnon: Helona, good for fresh fish.

FESTIVALS AND HOLIDAYS

The most important festivals are: Easter, in April, at the end of Holy Week; 1 May (Protomayia or May Day); Independence Day (25 March), celebrating the start of the rising against the Turks in 1821; the Feast of the Assumption (15 August); and Ohi Day (28 October), anniversary of the famous 'No!' (*ohi*), the reply supposedly given by Prime Minister Metaxas to Mussolini's ultimatum on that day in 1940.

ADDITIONAL INFORMATION

Languages

Apart from Greek, English and German are the languages most commonly understood or spoken by the islanders, plus, in the Ionian Islands, Italian.

Personal safety

Greece is a very safe country, and theft is rare. Driving a car, though, is something of a challenge, as many roads are potholed, in poor condition, and very slippery after rain. Greeks don't drive slowly … Watch out for bus drivers, who put their foot down even on narrow, winding roads.

Health

Before leaving for Greece, obtain an E111 form from your post office. This will entitle you to free *basic* health care abroad, but you may wish to consider private insurance to cover nursing fees, special tests and treatment, etc.

Electricity supply

220 v everywhere.

Post and telecommunications

Mail from the islands follows circuitous routes to its destination. In tourist hotspots and university towns a crop of Internet cafés has sprung up, making it possible to e-mail home. Public telephones use phone cards sold for €3 at street kiosks, offices of the OTE, mini-markets, etc.

All the photographs in this book are by Patrick de Wilde of Agence Photographique Hoa-Qui Distribution (www.hoaqui.com) except:

Bruno Pérousse/Hoa-Qui Distribution: pp. 10 (5th from left), 24–5, 49, 56, 57;
Sylvain Cordier/Hoa-Qui Distribution: pp. 18–19;
Philippe Royer/Hoa-Qui Distribution: p. 22;
Wotjek Buss/Hoa-Qui Distribution: pp. 26, 29 (top);
Christian Vaisse/Hoa-Qui Distribution: p. 55;
François La Treille/Hoa-Qui Distribution: p. 59;
Patrick Frillet/Hoa-Qui Distribution: pp. 60, 61, 146–7;
Jean-Michel Ruiz/Hoa-Qui Distribution: p. 145 (right).

Editor: Valérie Tognali
Art editor: Sabine Houplain
Design: François Supiot
Copy editor/proofreader: Isabelle Macé
Map: Cyril Süss
Production: Nicole Thiériot-Pichon
Photoengraving: SELE OFFSET (Turin)

First published by Editions du Chêne, an imprint of Hachette-Livre
43 Quai de Grenelle, Paris 75905, Cedex 15, France
Under the title *Les Iles Grecques*.
© 2004, Editions du Chêne-Hachette Livre
All rights reserved

English language translation produced by Translate-A-Book, Oxford

This edition published by Hachette Illustrated UK, Octopus Publishing Group,
2–4 Heron Quays, London, E14 4JP
English Translation © 2005, Octopus Publishing Group Ltd, London

ISBN-13: 978-1-84430-147-8
ISBN-10: 1-84430-147-8
Printed by Toppan Printing Co., (HK) Ltd.